The Essential Guide to Autophagy

Unlock Your Body's Natural Repair Mechanism to Weight Loss and Healing with Intermittent Fasting

© **Copyright 2018 - All rights reserved.**

The content contained within this book may not be reproduced, duplicated or transmitted without direct written permission from the author or the publisher.

Under no circumstances will any blame or legal responsibility be held against the publisher, or author, for any damages, reparation, or monetary loss due to the information contained within this book. Either directly or indirectly.

Legal Notice:

This book is copyright protected. This book is only for personal use. You cannot amend, distribute, sell, use, quote or paraphrase any part, or the content within this book, without the consent of the author or publisher.

Disclaimer Notice:

Please note the information contained within this document is for educational and entertainment purposes only. All effort has been executed to present accurate, up to date, and reliable, complete information. No warranties of any kind are declared or implied. Readers acknowledge that the author is not engaging in the rendering of legal, financial, medical or professional advice. The content within this book has been derived from various sources. Please consult a licensed professional before attempting any techniques outlined in this book.

By reading this document, the reader agrees that under no circumstances is the author responsible for any losses, direct or indirect, which are incurred as a result of the use of information contained within this document, including, but not limited to, — errors, omissions, or inaccuracies.

Table Of Contents

Introduction

Chapter One: Introduction to Autophagy

  What is Autophagy?

  Benefits of Autophagy
- It Can Be Life-Saving
- May Promote Longevity
- Better Metabolism
- Reduction of the Risk of Neurodegenerative Diseases
- Regulates Inflammation
- Helps Fight Infectious Diseases
- Better Muscle Performance
- Prevents the Onset of Cancer
- Better Digestive Health
- Better Skin Health
- Healthy Weight
- Reduces Apoptosis

  Kickstart Autophagy
- Aerobic Exercise
- Intermittent Fasting and Caloric Restriction
- Protein Fast
- Keto Diet
- Sleep is Essential

Chapter Two: Discovery of Autophagy

Chapter Three: Autophagy and Intermittent Fasting

Chapter Four: Methods of Fasting

  Dry Fasting
- Benefits
- Preparing for the fast

  16:8 Intermittent Fasting
- Benefits
- Cons
- Break the fast

- One Meal a Day
- 5:2 Diet
  - Benefits
- Multi-Day Water Only Fasts
  - Benefits
  - How to do this fast
  - What to expect?
  - Breaking the fast

Chapter Five: Selecting a Method of Fasting

- What is Your Regular Diet Like?
- Are You Comfortable with the Idea of Fasting?
- What is Your Daily Schedule?

Chapter Six: How to Break a Fast

Chapter Seven: What Can You Drink During a Fast?

- Baking Soda
- Glauber's Salts
- Herbal Teas
- Coffee
- Artificial Sweeteners
- Apple Cider Vinegar
- Mineral Water

Chapter Eight: Benefits and Drawbacks of Fasting

- Benefits of Fasting
  - Weight Loss
  - Sleep
  - Resistance to Illnesses
  - A Healthy Heart
  - A Healthy Gut
  - Tackles Diabetes

Reduces Inflammation
Promotes Cell Repair

Drawbacks of Fasting
Weight Management
Short-Term Side Effects
Long-Term Side Effects
Dangers of Dry Fasting

People Who Should Not Fast
Pregnant Women
People With Medical Conditions
Eating Disorders
After a Surgery
Afraid of Fasting

Fasting Safely
Experience and Duration
Health
Nutrition and Hydration
Relationship with Food

Chapter Nine: Common Mistakes to Avoid
An Excuse to Eat Junk Food
Restricting Calorie Intake
Training Harder and Eating Less
Obsessing Over Timings
Not Drinking Sufficient Water
Not Keeping yourself Busy
Abusing Stimulants
Mindful Eating
Ease into Exercising

Chapter Ten: Don't Believe these IF Myths

Myth #1: You gain weight if you skip breakfast

Myth #2: Frequent meals improve your metabolism

Myth #3: Small meals lead to weight loss

Myth #4: The brain needs glucose, all the time

Myth #5: Eat often for good health

Myth #6: Your body shifts to starvation mode

- Myth #7: Fasting leads to muscle loss
- Myth #8: It leads to overeating

Chapter Eleven: Frequently Asked Questions

- How much time does your body need to get used to fasting?
- What are the benefits of this diet?
- Is it okay to consume certain beverages while fasting?
- Can intermittent fasting be combined with any other diet?
- Who should not fast?

Chapter Twelve: Tips and Tricks

- Skip Breakfast
- No Snacks After Dinner
- Black Coffee Helps
- Drink Lots of Water
- Adherence
- Fast While You Work
- Calories
- Train Fasted
- Patience
- Have Plenty of Protein
- Don't Be Too Hard on Yourself
- Delayed Gratification
- Don't Ignore Your Body

Chapter Thirteen: 5:2 Diet Meal Plan

- Day One: Monday

- Day Two: Tuesday
- Day Three: Wednesday
- Day Four: Thursday
- Day Five: Friday
- Day Six: Saturday
- Day Seven: Sunday

Chapter Fourteen: 16:8 Sample Menu
- Day One: Monday
- Day Two: Tuesday
- Day Three: Wednesday
- Day Four: Thursday
- Day Five: Friday
- Day Six: Saturday
- Day Seven: Sunday

Chapter Fifteen: One Meal a Day Sample Plan
- Level One: High-Fiber Vegetables
- Level Two: Fats and Oils
- Level Three: Proteins
- Level Four: Carbohydrates
- Level Five: Low-Glycemic Index Foods
  - Meal One: Monday
  - Meal Two: Tuesday
  - Meal Three: Wednesday
  - Meal Four: Thursday
  - Meal Five: Friday
  - Meal Six: Saturday
  - Meal Seven: Sunday

Conclusion

Resources

Introduction

What if I told you that you could lose weight without having to drastically cut down on your daily food intake? That does sound nice. If you're trying to shed those extra pounds without opting for a crash diet, then this is the perfect book for you.

You will be able to improve your overall health and achieve your weight loss goals by following the protocols of intermittent fasting. Instead of worrying about what you eat and how many calories you consume daily, you will need to shift your focus to when you eat.

I want to thank you for choosing this book, *'Autophagy - What It Is and How to Utilize It'* and hope you find it informative and interesting in your quest to learn more about Autophagy.

Intermittent fasting has many benefits, but the one advantage that's noteworthy is autophagy. Autophagy is an internal mechanism that kickstarts the process of cellular regeneration and waste removal, which has a positive impact on your overall health. When autophagy is performing optimally, it ensures that your body is healthy and functions optimally.

In this book, you will learn about autophagy, the different benefits it offers, the mechanism of autophagy, about intermittent fasting, the benefits of intermittent fasting, the different protocols of intermittent fasting, the myths related to intermittent fasting as well as a sample diet plan for different types of intermittent fasting that will help you follow this diet.

If you are ready to learn more about this wonderful diet

and the helpful process it enables, then let us get started immediately and understand how it works and how you can benefit from it.

Thank you once again for choosing this book.

Chapter One:

Introduction to Autophagy

What is Autophagy?

Did you know autophagy is a natural process where your body starts to eat itself? Wait, before you jump to any conclusions about this process, let me assure you that it is all good. Autophagy is an internal process by which your body cleanses itself by getting rid of all damaged cells and toxins and helps regenerate new and healthy cells.

Over time, the cells in your body tend to accumulate different dead organelles, proteins as well as oxidized particles that tend to clog the inner mechanisms of your body. This toxic buildup can accelerate the process of aging, induce dementia and also increase the risk of cancer as well as all other diseases related to aging. Since a lot of the cells in your body, like the ones in the brain, need to last you a lifetime, your body has developed a unique system that helps it get rid of all the defective cells and helps it to defend itself against diseases. All in all, it is a natural defense mechanism.

Here is a simple analogy that will help you understand autophagy before we get into the technical aspects of this unique process.

Your body is quite similar to a kitchen. After you cook a meal, you do clean the countertop, throw away the leftovers and recycle some of the food, don't you? If you do all this, then you will be able to wake up to a clean kitchen. This is exactly how autophagy works in your body.

Now, think of the same situation, but you are older and not as efficient as you used to be. After cooking your meal, you might leave the remnants on the countertop. Some of this might get tossed into the garbage while the rest stays as is. The leftovers linger on the counter, in the garbage and the recycling bin. They never make it out of the door and into the dumpster. After a while, this leads to a build-up of toxic waste in your kitchen. The food starts to ferment on the floor, and all kinds of nasty odors are produced. Due to the fact that pollutants, as well as toxins, are continuing to build up, it becomes difficult to scrub up all the daily grime. This scenario is quite similar to what your body will be like when autophagy isn't working effectively.

Autophagy usually works in the background, and it helps with the regular maintenance of the body. Autophagy kicks in during a high-stress situation as a way to enhance your body's natural defense mechanism to resist diseases and boost longevity. You can even increase the body's autophagy mechanism and you will learn more about all this later on in the book.

Benefits of Autophagy

Autophagy helps maintain homeostasis. What is homeostasis? Balanced cellular function in the body is known as homeostasis. Homeostasis, as well as vibrant health, is the result of the p62 protein working its magic during autophagy. As a result of this, all the damaged cells that are accumulated in the body over time are removed, and this creates space for new cells to form.

This process does sound good, but how does autophagy benefit you? Here are the benefits of autophagy.

It Can Be Life-Saving

It might sound a tad dramatic, but it is quite true. It is scientifically proven. Autophagy's main purpose is life preservation. During times of severe stress like infection or even starvation, this process is kick-started, and it helps optimize the process of repair while reducing damage.

Intermittent fasting activates autophagy and can starve any infectious intruder of glucose. This reduces inflammation so that it is easier for the immune system to take necessary action and help repair the damage that this inflammation and infection has caused. In short, the autophagy mechanism has evolved in such a manner that it helps save energy and repair damage when energy is scarce, but it is also important for the immune system's defense mechanism to fight any illness.

May Promote Longevity

Anti-aging benefits certainly sound mythical, almost like a unicorn. Beauty isn't merely skin deep, and it runs deeper. Scientists discovered autophagy during the 50s, and since then there have been several studies that were and are still being conducted to understand the manner in which autophagy improves cellular function and health.

Instead of absorbing any new nutrients, during autophagy, cells tend to replace their damaged parts, get rid of any toxic material within and start to fix themselves. When the cells in the body begin to repair themselves, they certainly tend to work better, and they act like younger cells.

You might have noticed some people have a different biological age and a different chronological age. The toxic damage that your body experiences and its ability to repair this situation plays a significant role in these differences.

Better Metabolism

Autophagy is similar to a housekeeping service. Not only does it take the trash out, but also it replaces different vital cell parts like the mitochondria. Mitochondria are the powerhouse in a cell that not only burns fat and produces ATP, but is also your body's energy currency. Any buildup of toxins in the mitochondria doesn't just damage cells, and if these cells are destroyed proactively, it helps save future wear and tear of the cells.

Autophagy helps your cells function more effectively and efficiently, and it also helps synthesize new proteins. All this makes your cells quite healthy and this, in turn, improves your metabolism.

Reduction of the Risk of Neurodegenerative Diseases

Most of the diseases related to the aging of the brain take a long time to develop since the proteins present in and around the brain cells are misfolded, and they don't function like they are supposed to. As mentioned earlier, autophagy helps clean up all these malfunctioning proteins and reduces the accumulation of such proteins.

For instance, in Alzheimer's, autophagy removes amyloid and in Parkinson's it removes α-synuclein. There is a reason why it is believed that dementia and diabetes go hand in hand with each other as constantly high levels of blood sugar prevent autophagy from kicking in, and this makes it quite difficult for cells to get rid of the clutter.

Regulates Inflammation

Do you remember the story of Goldilocks? How she found the perfect bed and the perfect bowl of porridge - that's not too hot or too cold, but just perfect? Likewise, autophagy helps regulate inflammation, and it produces a "Goldilocks" amount of inflammation in the body by either boosting or quelling the response of the immune system according to what your body needs.

Autophagy can increase the presence of inflammation by increasing it when there is an alien body in the body by triggering the defense mechanism of the immune system. Usually, autophagy decreases inflammation from the response of your immune system by getting rid of antigens that trigger it unnecessarily.

Helps Fight Infectious Diseases

As I have already mentioned, autophagy helps trigger the immune response as and when necessary. The autophagy mechanism helps get rid of specific microbes that are directly present within the cells like Mycobacterium tuberculosis or viruses like HIV. Autophagy also helps remove the toxins that are produced because of infections, especially any illness that's foodborne.

Better Muscle Performance

Exercise results in slight microtears and slight inflammation of muscles and this needs to be repaired. The demand for energy increases due to this. The cells in your muscles respond to this by inducing autophagy to reduce the energy that's necessary to use the muscle, eliminate the damaged bits and improve the overall balance of energy to decrease the risk of any future damage.

Prevents the Onset of Cancer

Autophagy helps suppress the process that induces cancer like severe inflammation, instability in genomes and the DNA response to damage. Studies on mice, that have been genetically designed to suppress autophagy, have shown an increased rate of cancer. As cancer progresses, it might activate autophagy to generate alternate fuel or to even hide from the immune system, but all the research so far has only been on animals and not on human beings.

Better Digestive Health

The cells in the lining of the gastrointestinal tract are at work, all the time. A large portion of your feces is cells. When autophagy is activated, your digestive cells have an opportunity to repair, restore and clear themselves of any junk and reduce or trigger the immune system's reaction as needed.

Any chronic immune response in the gut can not only overwhelm your bowels, but it can also lead to inflammation within, so a chance to rest, repair and clean themselves is important for better digestive health. Autophagy gives your digestive system a much-needed respite from all the work it does.

Better Skin Health

The cells that are exposed on the body are vulnerable to a variety of damage from chemicals, air, light, humidity, pollution and all forms of physical damage. It's quite a surprise that we don't look worse for wear given all that we expose our skin to. When your skin cells start to accumulate damage and toxins, then they begin to age.

Autophagy helps repair and replace these cells, and it

makes your skin look fresh. Skin cells tend to engulf bacteria that can damage the body, so it is quintessential that you support them as they are clearing the clutter.

Healthy Weight

Here are a couple of benefits of autophagy that help you maintain a healthy weight.

Short periods of fasting help activate autophagy, burn fat, hold onto muscle mass and enable you to become lean and fit. It also reduces the chances of unnecessary inflammation that usually leads to weight gain. Autophagy helps reduce the levels of toxins in your body, and when this happens, the cells in your body will not retain a lot of fat.

Autophagy also supports your metabolic efficiency by repairing those parts of the cells that usually create and package proteins and synthesize energy, which is helpful when the cells need to start burning fat to provide energy.

Reduces Apoptosis

Apoptosis is programmed cellular death. When compared to autophagy, apoptosis is quite messy, and it also creates more garbage that needs to be cleaned up. To assist in this cleanup, your body triggers inflammation. The more cells that are repaired, the less effort your body needs to make to clean away old cells and produce new ones.

Renewal of tissues requires less inflammation, so your body starts to use that energy to replace those cells that require constant renewal, like the cells in your digestive system or skin. While some cells need to be renewed regularly, there are some that don't. An increased effort to repair with fewer cleanups is a great combination for your body to function optimally.

Kickstart Autophagy

Autophagy is a very important cellular process that provides a lot of physiological benefits when it is activated. Essentially there are two options in which you can activate autophagy - you can either induce stress, or you need to ingest something that kickstarts autophagy. There are different ways in which you can kickstart autophagy in your body. To cleanse the cells, reduce any inflammation and keep your body functioning optimally, here are some steps you can follow that will speed up the process of autophagy. Autophagy is your body's natural response to stress, so you need to trick your body into thinking that it is under a little stress.

Aerobic Exercise

Aerobic exercise helps kickstart autophagy in tissues present in the muscles as well as the brain. Exercise places prolonged stress on the cells and this, in turn, activates autophagy. Exercising will not only make you feel good, but it also improves your overall fitness and induces autophagy that ensures that all the cells in your body fully recover from the exercise. If you want to harness the benefits of autophagy, then include some physical exercise.

High-intensity interval training, also known as HIIT is a type of exercise that stimulates autophagy. Remember that autophagy is the response to stress, and HIIT induces the right amount of stress that activates autophagy without causing any damage. 20-30 minutes of HIIT will do the trick for your body.

Intermittent Fasting and Caloric Restriction

Intermittent fasting, as well as any form of caloric restriction, induces autophagy. Any shortage or even the lack of an influx of nutrients activates autophagy in the body. This helps with the recycling of any toxic cellular components in the body and ensures that all the cells are functioning properly and are in an energy converting mode. You can achieve this by either abstaining from food for a while or even reducing the food that you eat. Short-term fasts like the ones prescribed by intermittent fasting will help you achieve this.

The simplest way to kickstart autophagy is by following the protocols of intermittent fasting. If you fast for short durations, your body is tricked into thinking that it is under stress and it helps increase your body's autophagy response. You will learn more about intermittent fasting in the coming chapters.

Protein Fast

A protein fast helps do this as well. Once or twice a week, you should try to limit your protein intake to 15 grams per day. When you do this, it gives your body a chance to recycle proteins - this reduces inflammation and cleanses your cells without any loss of muscle. During this time, autophagy is triggered, and your body is forced to consume the proteins that aren't synthesized yet and get rid of all toxins.

Autophagy is a very important cellular process that provides a lot of physiological benefits when it is activated. Essentially there are two options in which you can activate autophagy - you can either induce stress, or you need to ingest something that kickstarts autophagy. In this section you will learn about the different ways in which you can activate autophagy in your body.

Keto Diet

The keto diet is a low-carb and a high-fat diet, so this diet will drastically reduce your intake of carbs while increasing your intake of fats. This change in the primary source of energy from glucose to fats is known as ketosis. This change that takes place is quite similar to the one that takes place when you are fasting, and this induces autophagy. The keto diet is a great option for all those people who aren't too comfortable with the idea of fasting.

Following a high fat and a low-carb diet like the keto diet helps activate autophagy. You must ensure that the primary macronutrient in your diet is fat. A diet like a keto diet gives your body a chance to kickstart autophagy. The natural shift that occurs in your body when your source of energy is changed from glucose to ketones (it occurs naturally during a fasted state) increases the process of autophagy.

Sleep is Essential

Even restorative sleep helps your body cleanse itself. Regulating your natural circadian rhythm and getting sufficient sleep naturally helps your body perform better. Autophagy occurs while you are asleep. The circadian rhythm not only helps regulate your sleep cycle, but it is also associated with autophagy. Our body's internal biological clock affects the rhythm of autophagy in your body, so sufficient sleep does help with autophagy.

Chapter Two:

Discovery of Autophagy

Yoshinori Ohsumi was awarded the Nobel Prize in Physiology or Medicine in 2016 for discovering the mechanisms of autophagy.

2016's Nobel Laureate is accredited with not just the discovery, but the elucidation of the mechanisms underlying autophagy - a primary process that's responsible for the degradation and the recycling of the components of cells.

Yoshinori Ohsumi was born in Fukuoka, Japan in the year 1945. In 1974, he acquired a Ph.D. from the University of Tokyo. He spent three years in the USA at the Rockefeller University, and after this, he returned to the University of Tokyo to start his research group in 1988. Since 2009, he has been a professor at the Tokyo Institute of Technology.

The term autophagy is derived from the Greek language - auto (it means self) and phagein (it means to eat). Therefore, autophagy quite literally means self-eating. This concept appeared for the first time during the '60s when researchers noticed that cells are capable of destroying their own components by enclosing them within membranes and forming a sack-like vesicle around them that helped transport them to a recycling component (known as lysosome) for degradation.

It was quite difficult to study this fascinating phenomenon since little was known until Yoshinori Ohsumi started his series of rather brilliant experiments from the early 1990s. He used baker's yeast to identify the genes that are necessary for autophagy and then went on to explain the mechanism responsible for autophagy in yeast and shows that a similar mechanism is present within human cells as well.

Ohsumi's research helped change the way we understand the manner in which cells recycle their contents. His discoveries paved the way to understanding the important role that autophagy plays in various physiological processes like the body's mechanism during starvation and its response to infection. Any harmful mutations in the autophagy genes can cause diseases, and this process is also involved in various severe conditions like cancer as well as neurological disorders.

During the mid-1950's, scientists noticed a new cellular component known as an organelle that contains enzymes that digest proteins, carbs and lipids. This specialized organelle is known as a "lysosome," and it acts as the compartment for cellular component's degradation. Christian de Duve, a Belgian scientist, discovered the lysosome and he was awarded the Nobel Prize in Physiology or Medicine in 1974.

Several observations showed that large portions of cellular content, as well as whole organelles, could be found within lysosomes. It seemed like the cell had a specific strategy to transport large cargo loads to the lysosome. Further analysis revealed that there is a specific type of vesicle that helps transport cellular cargo to the lysosomes for degradation. Duve coined the term autophagy to describe this process, and the new vesicles that were discovered were given the name autophagosome.

All cells have different compartments and a lysosome is one such compartment that contains certain digestive enzymes. An autophagosome, a new kind of vesicle, was also observed within this cell. Autophagosome engulf cellular contents like damaged proteins as well as organelles. Finally, it all fuses with the lysosome and all the cellular components are broken down into smaller bits. This process gives the cells certain necessary nutrients, and it also helps in cell renewal.

During the 1970s and 80s, researchers started to concentrate on another system that the body uses to degrade proteins known as Proteasome. In 2004, Aaron Ciechanover, Avram Hershko and Irwin Rose were given the Nobel Prize in Chemistry for "the discovery of ubiquitin-mediated protein degradation." The proteasome helps to degrade proteins efficiently, but it failed to explain how the cells usually get rid of larger proteins and worn-out organelles present in the body.

Ohsumi was quite active in different areas of research, but once he started his lab in 1988, his primary focus was on protein degradation in an organelle known as the vacuole that corresponds to the lysosome present in human cells. Yeast cells are comparatively easier to study and therefore are usually used as a model for human cells.

They are quite helpful when identifying the genes that play a critical role in intricate cellular pathways. Ohsumi faced a major challenge while working with yeast cells since these cells are tiny and it isn't easy to distinguish their inner structures under the microscope, and this made him uncertain about whether autophagy existed in this organism or not.

Ohsumi believed that if he can disrupt the degradation process within the vacuole when autophagy was active, then the autophagosome will accumulate within the vacuole and will become visible under a microscope. Therefore, he started to culture mutated yeast devoid of any vacuolar degradation enzymes and starved the cells to stimulate autophagy. The results obtained from this experiment were rather striking. Within a couple of hours, the vacuoles in the cells were filled with tiny vesicles that were not degraded.

The vesicles were autophagosomes, and this showed that autophagy did exist in yeast cells. What's even more important is that now he had discovered a method to identify and characterize the primary genes involved in this process. Ohsumi published his results about this breakthrough in 1992. His results encouraged him to study various yeast mutants, and he managed to identify 15 genes that are important for autophagy.

He took some of the specially engineered yeast strains that had accumulated autophagosomes during starvation. This accumulation would not occur if the genes necessary for autophagy were inactive. Ohsumi exposed the yeast cells to a chemical, which randomly introduces mutations to different genes, and then he induced autophagy into these cells, and his strategy certainly worked.

Within one year of this discovery that autophagy exists in yeast cells, Ohsumi managed to identify certain genes essential for autophagy. The results of all his subsequent experiments showed that autophagy is controlled by a variety of proteins and protein complexes that each regulate a different stage of the autophagosome initiation and formation.

After he managed to identify the machinery of autophagy in yeast cells, an important question was yet to be answered. Was there any other corresponding mechanism that controlled this process in other organisms? It soon became clear that a mechanism identical to the one in yeast takes place in human cells as well. Before Ohsumi's research, the tools that are necessary to study the importance of autophagy were not available, and now they were.

Thanks to Ohsumi's research and several others who followed his research, we are now certain that autophagy controls various physiological functions that are important wherein the cellular components must be degraded and then recycled.

Autophagy can provide the fuel for not just energy, but also supplies the building blocks that are necessary for the renewal of cellular components and it is, therefore, an important cellular response to any stress, like starvation. After the onset of an infection, autophagy helps get rid of the invading bacteria or virus.

Autophagy also helps in embryo development as well as cell differentiation. Autophagy is also shown to help counteract the effects of aging in cells. The concept of autophagy has been around for a while, but its primary importance came to light only due to Ohsumi's research.

Chapter Three: Autophagy and Intermittent Fasting

Do you know what the best thing about intermittent fasting is? Weight loss and better health are undoubtedly good reasons; however, the answer is autophagy. Do you know what autophagy is? Read on to learn more about autophagy and how intermittent fasting helps.

There are different reasons why people opt for intermittent fasting, and the reasons can range from weight loss to convenience. Restricting yourself to an eating window of just a couple of hours daily puts your body into a state of calorie deficit, but using intermittent fasting to lose weight is merely a partial benefit.

Juice cleanses and detox diets don't work. They are merely fad diets, and like all fads, they will fade away. There is nothing wrong with having a kale smoothie to flush the toxins out of your system; however, there is a better way to get rid of toxins. Our bodies can cleanse themselves, and it is via a process that you can fully control. All you need to do is trigger the self-cannibalism metabolism of your body. It might sound slightly scary, but it is quite natural and perfect for your overall health. Does that seem dubious? It isn't, and you can train your body to eat itself. It is known as autophagy, and it helps to cleanse your body. Apart from all the toxins in the body, there are plenty of dead and diseased cells as well.

In autophagy, your body gobbles up these cells and helps to make new ones in their place. You have to send your car for servicing from time to time, even if it functions well. You have to replace the oil in your car, and certain new parts have to be installed. In the same manner, your body needs to be serviced from time to time to make it more efficient. The faulty parts would need to be removed, and new ones put in their place. Well, autophagy does this for you.

Autophagocytosis is the technical term for autophagy. Autophagy might sound slightly scary, but it is an entirely natural process. It is a body mechanism that helps to disassemble our cells and get rid of all their components that are dysfunctional. It essentially means that your body is in a recycle mode and gets rid of all the waste that's accumulated within. Autophagy places your body in a catabolic state wherein it starts to break down its tissue instead of an anabolic state where it builds tissue.

There are plenty of benefits that autophagy offers. It helps to reduce inflammation in the body and strengthens your immune system. Autophagy also slows down the process of aging and suppresses the growth of cancerous cells and tumors. It also kills any infectious particles and toxins present in the body. The lack of autophagy leads to weight gain, laziness, impairment of the brain and high levels of cholesterol.

So, how does autophagy work? When your body triggers autophagy, the cells present in your body hunt for all the dead or malfunctioning cells and destroys them. Destroy might not be the right word; the healthy cells devour the unhealthy cells. It involves the creation of a double membrane around a cell that's going to be eaten, and it is known as an autophagosome. The diseased cell or the toxic protein is dissolved by the autophagosome, and it produces energy. How does your body regulate autophagy? The main triggers of autophagy are two types of protein enzymes known as mTOR and AMPK. mTOR is responsible for the growth of cells and the synthesis of proteins as well as anabolism. It helps to activate the insulin receptors in the body and helps the body create new tissue. AMPK activates a protein kinase that helps to balance energy levels when energy levels in the body are depleted.

How does intermittent fasting support autophagy? Intermittent fasting helps to trigger autophagy due to caloric deficiency. The reduction in the calorie intake helps the healthy cells to get rid of unnecessary proteins and break these down to release amino acids that provide energy. Intermittent fasting helps to improve your overall health, and prolongs your lifespan as well. Autophagy is the main reason for the benefits that intermittent fasting provides. Autophagy kicks in due to calorie restriction. You might wonder if a diet that prescribes small meals with little calorie intake might have similar benefits; however, it doesn't work like that. If you continuously provide your body with nutrition, it cannot enter autophagy. Two conditions are essential to autophagy. The first condition is the reduction of calorie intake and the second condition is a period of fast. When you fast, your body reaches for its reserves to provide energy. If you continuously supply it fuel, it doesn't have to process any fats or process any additional proteins. Your body is better off without any calories while you fast, instead of breaking the fast with a couple of calories and efficiently stopping autophagy. It is a good idea to follow the protocols of intermittent fasting, if not daily, then at least a couple of times a week.

Imagine if you have three square meals daily. You stop eating at 8 p.m., and you fast throughout the night. The first morsel of food you consume will be at 8 a.m. the following day. There is a gap of 12 hours between your meals; however, your body needs anywhere between 6 to 8 hours to fully digest the food you eat before it can shift into a fasted state. In practice, your fast doesn't start until the middle of the night, and you fast for only 6 hours. That isn't much time for your body to start autophagy. When your body is in a fed state, autophagy is low because of insulin and mTOR. Only when the fuel in your body decreases, does autophagy start. There is no fixed time for when autophagy starts. It varies according to the tissues in the body. As a rule of thumb, autophagy starts only when your insulin and mTOR levels are low. It doesn't happen when your body glucose levels are high. Your body needs to be in a state of mild ketosis with low levels of liver glycogen for this process to start. It can take anywhere between 12 to 16 hours for autophagy to set in; however, the process amps up after a couple of days of fasting.

However, it doesn't mean that you must starve yourself and stop eating altogether. If you do this, then you run the risk of starving your body, and it will negatively affect all the other activities you perform. Fasting doesn't lead to the loss of muscle, due to an increase in growth hormones and the production of ketones in the body. Autophagy is essential to maintain muscle mass.

Your body can enter into autophagy if you do the following.

Try to fast for a period of 14 to 16 hours daily to put your body in a fasted state. It will allow the depletion of glycogen reserves in your body and keep your body in a state of mild ketosis all day long. You must keep your insulin levels low in the blood. If you keep eating carbs or protein, then you will suppress autophagy; however, if you consume more fats, then you will contain the insulin response in your body and help to prolong the benefits of fasting. It might briefly stop autophagy, but it does put your body in ketosis. Ketosis helps to reduce inflammation and boosts the health of cells. Regardless of what you decide to do, don't binge on carbs. If you don't want to trigger the release of insulin and mTOR, then you must control your carb intake. Exercise also helps to stimulate autophagy in the body.

A little bit of self-destruction and stress are necessary to empower your body to function well. Self-destruction doesn't mean anything that puts you in mortal danger. It is a simple process that your body follows to cleanse and rid itself of additional proteins.

Chapter Four:

Methods of Fasting

Dry Fasting

Dry fasting is precisely what it sounds like - no food or water while you are fasting. It might sound quite strenuous, at least at first glance. Let me explain how this works and the benefits it offers, and you will undoubtedly change your mind. There are two things that you need to know about dry fasting, and they are that it has been around for centuries and people usually take it up for spiritual reasons. For instance, Muslims, during the month of Ramadan, follow a dry fast. The second thing is that when you follow a dry fast for short periods, it is not only effective but is quite safe too.

Benefits

- It helps lower inflammation in the body.

- It helps in the growth of new brain cells by promoting the release of the BDNF chemical. This chemical helps improve your memory, ability to learn, creates new neurons and also helps prevent the degeneration of brain cells.

- Dry fasting helps balance the levels of cholesterol in the body. It helps to increase the levels of good cholesterol or HDL and reduce the bad cholesterol or LDL levels in the body.

- It also helps regulate blood sugar levels in the body.
- Apart from all this, it also prevents the onset of osteoporosis.

Preparing for the fast

Dry fasting isn't something that you need to do for prolonged periods. If you extend it over 24 hours, then it will seriously harm your body. It's a good idea to start with 12 hours of dry fasting and slowly make your way up to a 24-hour fast. Also, don't attempt this fast for more than one day in a week.

You will need to prepare yourself for this fast, and it isn't something that you can jump into. Before you start your fast, you need to start increasing your water intake to keep your body hydrated. Since you will not be allowed to drink any water while fasting, you need to make sure that your body is hydrated and it can sustain itself during the fast.

Dry fasting is an intensive form of fasting when compared to other fasts. When you are following this fast, you must break your fast as soon as you start to feel dizzy, lightheaded or faint. Break your fast with a glass of lukewarm water with some lemon juice and honey. You can also have some probiotic drink like raw kefir water or sauerkraut juice. Prepare your gut before you start eating anything.

16:8 Intermittent Fasting

This is the most popular form of intermittent fasting. In this variation, you will be required to fast for 16 hours, and your feeding window extends to eight hours. Your body is fasting while you are sleeping. Therefore, it makes perfect sense to include any sleeping time to the fasting period. Within the feeding window that this diet provides, you can squeeze in two hearty meals. The 16/8 method is also called Leangains and is perhaps the most famous variation of intermittent fasting. Martin Berkhan, a fitness expert, popularized Leangains. It is not only the most popular but the simplest form of intermittent fasting as well. Skipping your breakfast and having your first meal at noon and your dinner at 8 p.m. in the night is an example of the lean gains method. You will be fasting for 16 hours daily.

If you are not an early riser or are in the habit of regularly skipping your breakfast, then this method will be quite easy for you to follow. During the fasting period, you are free to consume all sorts of beverages that don't have any calories in them, so you can have plenty of herbal teas, water, black coffee and green tea. If your primary goal is weight loss, then you must stay away from all processed and junk foods. Gorging on any kinds of unhealthy junk will defeat the purpose of fasting all day long. If you want this diet to work, then you must stick to healthy and wholesome foods. Depending on the schedule you are used to, you can make adjustments to your eating window time.

Benefits

When it comes to this form of fasting, you don't have to plan too much. You can create your own set of rules and follow a timing pattern that suits your needs. If you want to start your fast from night until noon, then feel free to do so. You don't have to worry about counting calories or even the macros you consume. As long as you fast for 16 hours and then eat a healthy meal, you are good to go.

There are no dietary restrictions about your carb intake. You can consume carbs if you feel like you need them to maintain your energy; however, it doesn't mean that you binge on sugary and carb-laden treats after breaking your fast.

Even when you aren't counting calories and aren't tracking the macros you consume, you will start to lose weight. This form of intermittent fasting turns your body into a fat burning machine. Your body shifts into ketosis during the fasting period and starts burning its internal reserves of fat to provide constant energy, so you will feel quite energetic throughout the day even when you don't eat anything.

This method is quite economical as well. By following this pattern of eating, you can reduce your food expenditure. You will be able to save a handful of dollars every month, and over a period, it will add up to a rather handsome sum.

Cons

This form of intermittent fasting can be tricky for all those who aren't used to fasting daily. You will need to fast between 14 to 16 hours per day on this method. So you will need to get yourself, and your body, used to this method of fasting. Fasting for prolonged periods can cause hunger pangs, and this can cause mood swings. Some people also complain about headaches and nausea. These side effects are common during the initial days of fasting and will fade away slowly. They occur since your body is getting used to a new diet.

Some people can be shocked about the pace at which they are losing weight. This method promotes quick weight loss within a short period, so prepare yourself for all this before you decide to go ahead with it.

You might feel quite tempted to eat something while fasting, and if you do give in to your urges, you might experience some guilt later. Thus, you need to work on developing self-control, if you want this diet to be successful for you.

Break the fast

Your body needs a little insulin to transport different nutrients from one cell in the body to another; however, if there is any drastic spike in your levels of insulin, it can lead to drowsiness as well as lethargy, so it is a good idea that the first meal that you consume after breaking the fast is a small one and is low-glycemic. A low-glycemic meal is not rich in carbs, and it helps your body to get into the groove of eating and digesting food after a period of fasting. It also ensures that your body stays in a semi-fasted state because of the lack of any spike in blood sugar levels. You also don't have to worry about losing any muscles since your body is only burning ketones to provide energy and isn't cannibalizing itself. Fasting shifts your body into ketosis and having MCTs or bone broth prevents self-cannibalization. Here are a couple of examples of a low-glycemic meal. You can have two eggs with half an avocado, a handful of spinach and a few nuts. You can also have a can of sardines along with a light salad with an olive oil dressing.

Did you know that it is easier for your body to digest lean proteins like fish or eggs instead of red meats? So, ensure that you break your fast with a light meal before you decide to eat any red meats. If you do want to have some meat, then you can include that in your second meal.

Alternatively, you can also break your fast by eating fruits. Fruits are full of fructose, and your liver is the only organ in your body that can metabolize this form of sugar. Your body cannot use this sugar to replace any depleted muscle glycogen, and the liver can hold onto only 100 to 150 grams of glycogen. This reserve of glycogen is rather quickly depleted while fasting especially if the fast goes on for 16 hours. So when can you eat fruits? The best time to eat fruits is when your glycogen store is almost empty - after you exercise or after you end your fast. If your liver has sufficient glycogen stored within it, then any intake of additional glycogen will only lead to an increase in fat reserves, and it will defeat the purpose of fasting altogether. It is a better idea to not break your fast by eating fruits. Fruits contain sugars, and if you want to stay in ketosis, then you don't need any sugars. If you want to eat fruits, then always opt for those that are rich in fiber like pears, berries or even apples.

One Meal a Day

The popularity of intermittent fasting is rapidly increasing these days. One method of intermittent fasting that is steadily gaining popularity is the One Meal a Day diet or the OMAD diet. Fasting is a very powerful tool that helps optimize your body's performance, especially when you fast for extended periods, it tends to have a positive effect on not just your body but your mind too.

The OMAD protocol is designed such that the fasting ratio that you must follow is 23:1. It simply means that you will be fasting for 23 hours in a day and your eating window is restricted to about one hour. In this one hour, you can have one large meal that's rich in all the nutrients that your body needs. If you are trying to burn fat, enhance your mental clarity and reduce the time that you spend thinking about, planning and eating food, then this is a great diet for you.

This method of fasting alternates between periods of eating and fasting. This method of fasting drastically reduces your eating window unlike the other forms of intermittent fasting. While following this method of fasting, you must ensure that you are consuming your daily dose of calories within that one meal and you are fasting for the rest of the day. This method of intermittent fasting offers all the benefits of fasting and will certainly simplify your daily schedule. I suggest that the ideal time to break your fast is between 4 to 7 p.m.

When you do this, you will be effectively giving your body the time that it needs to start digesting its last meal before you go to sleep.

From an evolutionary perspective, human beings are not designed to eat three meals per day. The bodies of our ancestors were used to functioning effectively even when food was scarce. Intermittent fasting like OMAD tends to kickstart different cellular functions in the body that are necessary to improve your overall health. It might seem quite intimidating to start with this form of fasting. There are three rather simple tips that you can follow to make the transition to this diet easy on your body.

The first thing you need to do is to ensure that you slowly reduce your carb intake. If you want to maximize the results this diet offers and don't want to experience any symptoms of carb withdrawal, then you need to gradually reduce your carb intake before you start this diet. When you are eating carbs, your body keeps a store of glycogen within it. If there is an endless supply of glycogen, then it will keep using the immediately available resources and will not use the stored glucose. All this leads to weight gain. The idea of fasting is to encourage your body to burn its reserves before accepting any new glucose into the body. If you can effectively shift your body into ketosis, you will make your body a fat burning machine.

The second thing that you need to do is give your body the time it needs to get used to this protocol. From eating three meals a day along with snacks, you need to condition your body to eat only one meal per day. This might not seem like much, but it is a major change for your body, so the best way to go about it is to slowly reduce the number of meals you eat while increasing the gap between two meals. Stop snacking and start eating nutrient dense foods to regulate your hunger.

Another simple way in which you can make this diet easier on your body is to consume some caffeine. A morning cup of coffee (without any milk and sugar) will make you feel full for longer and will keep your hunger pangs at an arm's distance. You will learn more about the different tips that you can follow to manage your hunger later on in this book.

5:2 Diet

It is a distinct method, and you will be fasting on every alternate day according to the protocols of this technique. There are a couple of different variations of this form of intermittent fasting. One variation of this diet prescribes that you must have 500 calories on every alternate day and regular meals on all the other days. You can observe a strict fast if you can on every alternate day. All this solely depends on your level of comfort and nothing else. If a strict fast, sounds a little extreme for you, you can opt for any other variation. By following this protocol, you will be required to fast for two days in a week and the fasting days must not be consecutive. It is also known as the 5:2 method. Michael Mosley popularized this diet.

So, when you are following the protocols of this diet, you don't have to follow a rigorous fast, and instead, you merely need to reduce your calorie intake to about 500 calories for two days in a week. Try not to fast on consecutive days since it is not recommended, so as long as you space these days correctly, you are good to go. For instance, you can decide to fast on Monday and Thursday and eat normally on Tuesday, Wednesday, Friday, Saturday and Sunday.

Benefits

If you are looking for a diet that is sustainable not just for the time being but also in the long run, then this is a good option.

- It helps control blood sugar levels and is specifically a good fit for all those who have diabetes.

- It also gives your digestive system the much-needed respite from all the constant work it does.

- The 5:2 diet is very simple to follow, and with a little planning, it is quite helpful. You merely need to plan for your meals ahead of time and then work accordingly.

- On the days of your fast, ensure that you are not exceeding the 500-calorie limit and are drinking plenty of water.

- It is a great fit for all those who don't like the idea of fasting daily and don't like to follow strict fasts that are devoid of food.

Multi-Day Water Only Fasts

A three-day water fast is quite good for all those who are used to the one-day fast or the 24-hour fasting protocol. This is an extended and an intensive version of the 24-hour protocol.

Benefits

You need to prepare yourself mentally as well as physically for this form of fasting. Many people are scared to attempt anything like this, so before you get put off by the notion of a three-day water only fast, let me tell you the benefits it offers.

The human digestive system usually works without any respite; it is on duty around the clock. A fast gives your body the rest it deserves, and it allows your digestive system to cleanse, repair and heal itself. This fast helps remove a lot of the stored toxins from your body.

It also improves immunity and prolongs the longevity of the cells in the body.

This is an effective means to lose weight. You can lose up to 5 pounds within three days while fasting, but remember that you will gain it back as soon as you revert to your old eating habits. You need to follow a healthy and a well-balanced diet plan if you want to maintain your weight loss. Most of the weight that you lose will be water weight, so be careful that you don't dehydrate yourself.

While fasting, you can observe your mind and the way it

usually behaves. This will give you an insight into your food cravings and habits. It will also help you become mindful of what you eat and when you eat.

This fast also offers certain spiritual benefits. Think of it as a means to cleanse your body, mind, and soul. It is believed that fasting offers time for spiritual and emotional introspection. Therefore, it is no wonder that this fast is often performed for spiritual reasons in different religions.

How to do this fast

During this fast, you must only drink water for three days or 72 hours. You cannot have any solid food or any other liquids that contain any calories or nutrition. It is as simple as that. You can have boiled water if you want. Make it a point to drink at least three liters of water per day. Drinking warm water is a good idea since it helps cleanse the body internally.

What to expect?

When you are attempting this form of fasting, you will notice a couple of things in your body's reaction. We are all used to eating multiple meals in a day, and the sudden withdrawal of food can lead to weakness, dizziness, nausea or even headaches. These are quite natural and are bound to happen. At times, you will feel quite energetic and at times quite tired. The key is to not exert yourself too much and pace yourself as much as possible. This fast lasts for three days, so try not to tire yourself out. Get plenty of rest and don't exercise during this period. Fluctuations in energy are common, and you don't have to be worried about it. If you notice any severe reactions, then stop the fast and consult a doctor immediately.

To overcome any sudden pangs of hunger, try to drink a glass of water and count until 20 and the hunger pang will pass you by. If you constantly feel hungry, then discontinue this fast. In most cases, it usually isn't a serious issue.

You might start craving for food, and that's quite common too. Try to ignore this and concentrate on something else to take your mind off of hunger. You can even make a list of foods that you want to eat once you break the fast to distract yourself.

It is a physical cleansing time for your body, and your body starts expelling all the toxins stored within it during this time. You might notice a thick coating on your tongue while fasting, but you will only need to brush once to get rid of it.

Doctors usually prescribe an enema during this fast to get rid of toxins that are stored within the large intestine.

Acidity is quite common too, and you can overcome it by drinking some water with salt dissolved in it. It might cause you to vomit immediately, but it is good for your body. You need to remember that these things are quite common and you must prepare yourself to deal with them.

Breaking the fast

Slowly ease yourself back to your usual eating schedule. Don't start eating food as soon as you break this fast, and pace yourself when you do.

On the first day of breaking your fast, drink lemon or orange juice three to five times a day. You can add some honey to it to ease your digestive system to its usual routine.

On the second day, you can have light vegetable soups or broths, coconut water, and other fruits juices.

On the third day, have fruits and boiled vegetables, and from the fourth day, you can go back to eating the way you normally do. Ensure that you are eating well-balanced and healthy meals to avoid any weight gain and to maintain your weight loss.

Chapter Five:

Selecting a Method of Fasting

Now that you are familiar with different methods of fasting, the benefits that they offer and their potential drawbacks, the next step is to select a method of fasting. As you are aware, there are plenty of options to choose from, so how do you select one of these methods? If you can answer the three simple questions discussed in this chapter, you will know your answer.

Before you select a specific method, you need to understand the importance of selecting a specific method of fasting. So why is it so important to select the right method of fasting? You need to select a method that works well for you since doing this will increase the chances of success with your diet. It isn't just about that, though. Selecting the right method also improves your chances of following through with the diet and reduces the chances of you quitting.

If the option that you select is a good fit for your lifestyle and it doesn't feel like you need to make any extra effort to follow it, it is quite likely that you will stick to it. If you try to follow a fasting protocol that doesn't fit into your daily schedule, then that's just added stress. God knows that we all have sufficient things to worry about and we certainly don't need another reason to stress about, so here are the three questions that you need to ask yourself before you decide to opt for a specific form of fasting.

What is Your Regular Diet Like?

If your regular diet is full of processed foods, carbs and sugars, then fasting is a rather tricky change to get used to. Any diet that's rich in sugars and carbs is addictive, and if you decide to start fasting by opting for a stringent protocol like dry fasting or 16:8 fasting, then you will experience a couple of withdrawal symptoms. It becomes difficult to stick to a fasting schedule once you start to experience such symptoms. If this happens, then the chances of prematurely giving up on the diet increase exponentially.

So, it is always a good idea to opt for a fasting protocol that corresponds with your sleeping schedule. If you are opting for the 16:8 method, then most of your fasting period will be during your sleep, and it becomes easier to fast. You can gradually increase the duration of the fast.

This is one of the main reasons why it is better to start fasting gradually instead of going cold turkey. Unless you are an all or nothing sort of person, then I suggest that you gradually allow your body to get accustomed to the idea of fasting. You can start with a gradual fasting protocol like the 5:2 diet before you attempt any strict fast.

You need to prepare your body and mind for a fast. If you are used to a sugar and carb-rich diet, then slowly start by eliminating sugars and carbs from your diet and substitute them with healthier eating options like proteins and healthy fats. Once you start eliminating unhealthy foods from your diet, the next step is to slowly start increasing the time between your meals.

If you are used to constantly snacking, slowly eliminate the number of snacks you have and increase the duration between meals. Remember that it is all about getting your body used to this diet. Work with yourself slowly instead of going cold turkey.

A radical approach will not do your body any good, and you need to start slowly. You can obtain all the benefits of intermittent fasting without causing any harmful hormonal imbalances in your body. When you follow the protocols of this diet properly, you can shed all the excess pounds you want to. You can follow any of the other approaches as well if you aren't new to fasting.

The rules of fasting are quite simple. You must fast for two or three days in a week and make sure that you don't fast on any consecutive days. For instance, you can fast on Tuesday, Thursday, and Saturday. On the days you fast, keep your exercise protocol light - you can do some basic cardio or even some yoga. Make sure that your fasting period doesn't exceed 12-16 hours.

On the days when you don't fast, if you want to take up any high-intensity exercises, you should eat normally to maintain your energy levels. Always keep your body hydrated, and you can even have calorie-free beverages on your fasting days. If you decide to fast for two days a week, after two weeks, you can add another day to it.

Are You Comfortable with the Idea of Fasting?

Fasting is as much a physical concept as it is a psychological one, so ask yourself how comfortable you are with the idea of fasting. Are you okay with the idea of going an entire day without eating or are you comfortable with fasting for only a couple of hours? There are some who aren't comfortable with the idea of fasting for an entire day, and prefer shorter fasts, so the best way to figure this out is by testing yourself. Try to fast for twenty hours (without eating anything), and then the dry fast or even a 16:8 method will not be a challenge for you; however, if you like the idea of fasting where you are allowed to eat something, then opt for the one meal a day or the 5:2 fasting option.

Ensure that you take notice of how you feel while fasting. If you feel like it is quite a struggle and that you are uncomfortable, then chances are that you will not be able to adhere to a rigorous fasting routine, so stick to a shorter fasting window. It all depends on your level of comfort. If you are not comfortable with it, then please don't attempt it. If you want this diet to be sustainable for you in the long run, then you need to be comfortable with it.

What is Your Daily Schedule?

Fasting is quite easy to follow if you have a busy schedule. If you are preoccupied with a lot of other activities like your work, then you will not have any time on hand to think about fasting or even any hunger pangs. If you are used to exercising in the morning, then you need to opt for a fasting schedule that allows you to have a snack after your exercise.

Working out will certainly increase your appetite, and you will need to replenish the calories that you burn to assist in quick recovery. If you are used to skipping breakfast or don't like eating breakfast, then you can opt for the 16:8 protocol.

As I mentioned, you need to select a fasting method that is a good fit for you. If the fasting protocol seems difficult to you, then don't forget that you have the option of customizing it according to your schedule. This is perhaps the best thing about intermittent fasting. You will find something that's a good fit for you and you will be able to follow it without any difficulty. Remember that with intermittent fasting, you neither have to give up on your lifestyle or your diet to attain your health and weight loss goals.

Chapter Six: How to Break a Fast

Now that you are prepared to get started with intermittent fasting or any of the protocols of fasting, you need to learn about the different ways in which you can break your fast. In this section, I will introduce you to a whole range of healthy practices that you can follow while breaking your fast, so you do it in the right manner.

The first thing that you need to keep in mind while fasting is that you need to lose the "I can come up with a temporary solution" attitude. This is certainly not the best way to go about fasting or even following any other diet. There are a couple of things that may have prompted you to opt for fasting. Maybe you want to improve your overall health, meet your weight loss goals or even boost your body's metabolism. Regardless of the reason that made you opt for fasting, you need to keep a couple of things in mind before you break your fast. You might be wondering why you need these "rules."

Well, here are the reasons why you need to follow a couple of guidelines whenever you break your fast.

While you are fasting, the metabolism in your body goes through several hormonal and physiological changes. For instance, there is a spurt in the production of growth hormones, an elevation in luteinizing hormones, and autophagy is kick-started. While you are fasting, your body tends to be in ketosis, and this encourages your body to start producing ketones by burning fatty acids that are stored within.

The most important change of all is that when you don't eat anything for prolonged periods, then your digestive system starts to acclimatize itself to this.

If you eat anything and everything that you feel like as soon as the fast ends, then you will increase the stress on your gut and it results in inflammation. To avoid this, you need to be careful about the foods that you eat while breaking your fast.

What shouldn't you eat when you are breaking your fast? If you start eating foods that are rich in carbs, it leads to sudden weight gain because your body starts to retain sodium. While fasting, your body starts to expel a lot of water and if you start stuffing yourself up with all carb-rich foods, then it leads to antidiuresis of two important minerals - sodium and potassium. When this happens, it leads to bloating, and your energy levels will start to plummet as well.

Therefore, it is prudent that you ease your body from fasting into eating by consuming the right foods while breaking the fast. There is another factor that you need to consider, and that's the duration of your fast. If you are ending a 5-day fast, then you must be more patient with your body than while following a 5:2 day pattern of eating.

Let me start with a common scenario of fasting where you will need to fast for anywhere between 16 to 18 hours a day. Now imagine that you are almost done with fasting and you are close to the finish line. While you are fasting, you are allowed to consume all non-caloric beverages like water, herbal teas, black coffee and such. Now that it is time to break the fast, you need to consume foods that will slowly stimulate your digestive system without secreting any insulin.

Your best option in such a situation is to consume some apple cider vinegar. It helps neutralize and balance the pH levels in your body and kills any bad bacteria in the gut, stabilizes the blood sugar levels and also improves your overall health. You can also consume a tablespoon of apple cider vinegar while fasting to curb any hunger pangs and to feel refreshed. I suggest that it is better to drink this right before you break your fast. Here is a simple concoction that you can drink before you decide to eat any solid food. In one glass of lukewarm water, add two tablespoons of raw apple cider vinegar, squeeze in half a lemon, a pinch of cinnamon powder and add some sea salt or pink Himalayan sea salt to it.

If you aren't too keen on drinking apple cider vinegar, then remove that one ingredient and drink the rest. Lemon juice has citric acid in it, and this acid helps secrete digestive enzymes in your gut and prepares it for all the food that you are about to consume.

What can you drink when you are breaking the fast? Once you drink the above-mentioned concoction, try having some bone broth. Bone broth is a superfood, and it is quite nourishing for your body. It is full of collagen and electrolytes. Drinking some bone broth makes it easier for your body to absorb all the electrolytes and minerals from the meal you are about to eat. When you are fasting, your gut is on a self-cleanse and detox mode. You need to prepare it to absorb food so that you get all the nourishment from it.

If your fast extends over twenty hours, then have some light soup or bone broth before consuming any solid food. Do the same thing even if your fast was only for sixteen hours. You need to understand that your gut is cleansing itself for more than 14 hours and if you immediately eat solid food, then it can cause inflammation in your gut. If you don't want to have any bone broth, then you can have some fish broth. Making fish broth is quite easy. All those bits of the fish that you usually discard, you need to make a broth with it and a couple of other seasonings to make it fragrant and flavorful. Adding cinnamon to it will elevate the flavor profile of the broth and will speed up the absorption of nutrients in your gut.

When you are undergoing a fast, your body is in ketosis. If weight loss is your primary reason for opting for fasting, then it makes sense that you try and keep your body in ketosis even after you break the fast. If you don't have any bone broth on hand, but you want to give your body some instant energy without shifting out of ketosis, then you can have some MCT oil.

MCTs are readily converted into energy since they are pure fatty acids that are directly absorbed into your bloodstream and they bypass your liver altogether. This is very helpful since it helps you stay in ketosis for longer and your body continues to burn calories even when you aren't fasting. After you drink the glass of lemon water and bone broth, you need to give your body about 20 minutes to get prepared for the food you will consume. Giving it this prep time enables it to absorb nutrients effectively.

Chapter Seven: What Can You Drink During a Fast?

Well, now that you are aware of the different methods of fasting, the next step is to help you understand about the beverages that you can consume without breaking your fast. If you are following any of the protocols of intermittent fasting, then you must try to avoid any intake of calories for a specific period. For instance, if you opt for the 16:8 method, then you cannot eat or drink anything that has any calories in it during the fasting period. If you are following a diet like the 5:2 diet, then you are required to fast only on two days. Regardless of the method of fasting that you opt for, you must be aware of the beverages that you can consume to keep hunger at bay. Once your body is in a fasted state, then your body's physiology shifts into a state of mild ketosis and this increases your ability to burn fat and suppress your appetite, so the longer you fast for, the deeper the ketosis will be.

So, what can you drink while you are fasting without breaking your fast? The list of items discussed in this section will not only increase the effectiveness of the fast but will also increase the level of cellular detoxification and help cleanse your gut.

Baking Soda

Baking soda is commonly used in cooking, but it has several health benefits to offer. It helps with several digestive issues like constipation and bloating, it helps kill any bad bacteria and parasites present in the gut, helps reduce fatigue and tiredness of muscles, stabilizes the pH level in the gut and neutralizes acidity.

You need to add a teaspoon of baking soda to a glass of water and consume it if you want to improve your overall health and the physical performance of your body. An important thing that you need to keep in mind while fasting is that you need to keep your levels of electrolytes in check since they are constantly flushed out with water and other minerals.

100% sodium bicarbonate is known as baking soda, and it is a simple means of getting the necessary sodium into our body while fasting. Well, to be honest, it doesn't taste all that good, but it does help curb hunger, so you can forget about any hunger pangs and continue working as usual.

Glauber's Salts

If your primary reason for fasting is to promote cellular health and improve your overall health, then consuming Glauber's salts during the fasting window is a good idea. It is usually known as sodium sulfate decahydrate. Glauber's salts are used as a mild laxative, to help with bowel movements. Adding 5 to 20 grams of this salt to water can help relieve constipation, reduce bloating and it also helps to clean the digestive tract. Consuming more than 20 grams will lead to dehydration and diarrhea. So, be careful while you are adding this to water.

Herbal Teas

Herbal teas not only taste great, but they are also a great means to keep hunger at bay when you are fasting. Not just this, but they also have certain medicinal benefits to offer. Here are the benefits that different herbal teas offer.

If you have an upset stomach or have any trouble sleeping, then a cup of chamomile tea will help with these issues. Peppermint helps improve digestion, reduces muscle pain and helps manage inflammation. Jasmine tea helps to reduce cholesterol, reduces the risk of diabetes and it also strengthens the immune system. After water, green tea is believed to be the healthiest drink of all. It is rich in polyphenols that help improve heart and brain health. It also helps to speed up the process of fat burning. Black tea is rich in certain compounds that are good for your heart's health, digestion, and it also reduces stress.

A cup of herbal tea has less than eight calories, and you can safely consume it without breaking your fast; however, you must not brew teas with any fruits, berries or any other form of seasonings that are filled with carbs, if you don't want to break your fast. Consuming anything with sugar in it will prevent autophagy from kicking in.

Coffee

Coffee is the easiest and perhaps the most effective way to suppress hunger while fasting. Caffeine in it gives you instant energy that helps you focus better, and it also gives your fat burning mechanism a much-needed boost.

Apart from this, there are several other benefits that coffee offers. It helps regulate your blood sugar, maintains your count of polyphenol, and it also reduces the risk of Alzheimer's. It is not only good for your brain's health, but it also works wonders for your mitochondria. Mitochondria are the powerhouse of cells, and they help with better energy generation.

If you don't want to break your fast, then you should drink only black coffee. You can add a pinch of stevia to sweeten it or even some cinnamon to spice it up; however, don't keep adding stevia to it. I suggest that drinking black coffee without any additions is the best way to go about it. Try avoiding any of the instant coffee mixers since they usually have added substances that will break your fast, so please read the list of ingredients carefully before you reach for a cup of instant coffee.

It is a good idea to drink coffee to keep hunger at bay, but that doesn't mean that you should keep drinking coffee all the time. Be mindful of the amount of caffeine you are consuming. Coffee is a diuretic, and if you aren't careful, it can lead to dehydration. If you have anything more than two to four cups of coffee, it can lead to caffeine intolerance and even higher levels of cortisol. A high level of cortisol means that your stress levels will increase and it will make you catabolic, so if you are drinking coffee and you want to drink it regularly, regulate your intake of caffeine. A safe option is to choose decaf instead of the regular blends.

What about having bulletproof coffee while fasting? People frequently wonder if they can add some butter to their coffee while following the bulletproof style of fasting. Pure fats like butter, MCT oil and coconut oil will not raise your blood sugar, and it can keep your body in a semi-fasted state. The fat that you consume will not cross the blood-brain barrier, and it will seem like you haven't had anything to eat. It might seem quite nice, at least in theory, but if you do this, then it will block autophagy.

Since you are fasting to speed up the process of autophagy, then you need to do everything that you can to ensure that your body stays in a fasted state for as long as possible. Even consuming as little as fifty calories will shift your body from a fasted to a fed state. When this change occurs, then your body will stop autophagy, and the process of self-digestion of damaged cells will stop. That being said, I am not saying that this is a bad thing since you will be getting the energy that you need while in ketosis, but you will certainly be missing out on the benefits that autophagy offers like detoxification of your body. At this point, you need to think about your reasons for choosing an intermittent fasting protocol.

If your purpose for fasting is to lose weight and if adding butter or MCT oil to your cup of fix-me-up will get you through the fast then do so; however, you must remember that you will need to consume as little calories as possible, so if you think that you can dunk an entire stick of butter into the coffee, then you are mistaken. This will give you at least 500 calories to work with, and that's unnecessary.

If your primary reason for fasting is to cleanse your body from all the toxins building up within and to reduce inflammation, then, in my opinion, it is a good idea to not consume any beverages with added calories while fasting. Stick to mineral water, black coffee, herbal teas, and natural salts.

Artificial Sweeteners

This brings me to another common question - can you add any artificial sweeteners to your beverages while fasting?

The answer to this question is - it depends on the kind of sweeteners you are using, your reasons for intermittent fasting and the way your body reacts to these sweeteners. Usually, most sweeteners tend to have some hidden carbs in them. Maltodextrin, dextrose, and sucralose are examples of sweeteners with carbs in them, and it is best that you don't consume any of these when you are fasting. There are natural sweeteners like stevia that don't raise your blood sugar or insulin count, and it makes them a safe option.

However, you must still be aware of the way in which your body responds to these sweeteners. Stevia certainly doesn't have any added calories in it, but it is certainly sweeter than regular table sugar, and it can induce a placebo-like effect on your body in regards to your insulin response. Your taste buds will be tricked due to the sweetness of it, and it can take you out of the fasted state you are in. Technically, it doesn't have any calories, but your mind is a very powerful tool, and if it thinks that it is having something sweet, it will respond to it the way it responds to regular sugar, so you need to monitor the way your body reacts to it before you start adding it to your meals.

I suggest that it is a good idea to avoid all sweeteners while fasting. It is not that big of a deal, and if you want to, you can always experiment with a couple of options before coming to any conclusions about it.

Apple Cider Vinegar

While you are fasting, there is another great drink that you can consume to get through the fast without kicking yourself out of the fasted state. This wonderful drink is apple cider vinegar. It not only makes for a great dressing, but it is safe to drink in a diluted form. It has several anti-bacterial and anti-inflammatory compounds present in it. The acidic compounds present in it will help regulate the pH levels of your body. There are no calories as such in apple cider vinegar, and it has several other important minerals like potassium, magnesium, and iron in it. This is perfect to consume to ensure that your electrolyte levels are well balanced and that your body isn't dehydrated.

You need to add a tablespoon of it to a glass of water and drink it. It also helps curb hunger while giving you an energy boost. It is a good idea to break your fast with a glass of this concoction before you start eating anything. It helps activate the functions of your gut and helps prepare it for the food you are about to consume. Apple cider vinegar is known to kill the bad bacteria that are present in the gut.

Also, adding it to sparkling water makes for a tasty drink. To ensure that you are not halting autophagy in your body, it is ideal that you don't consume anything more than one or two tablespoons of apple cider vinegar at any given point of time.

As I mentioned, you can drink this while fasting, but you can also use it to break your fast. In a glass of lukewarm water, add a little lemon juice and apple cider vinegar to it and guzzle it down. If you do this, you will essentially be preparing your gut for the eating window.

Mineral Water

Well, let us not forget that water is perhaps the most important drink that you should be drinking. You can have regular, sparkling or even mineral water. Mineral water like Perrier is enriched with a couple of minerals that are good for your body.

Drink a lot of water to ensure that your body is thoroughly hydrated and you don't face the risk of dehydration. While you are fasting, your body tends to keep flushing out water, so you need to keep replacing it.

Also, drinking water helps curb any hunger you might feel. To prevent any imbalance of electrolytes in your body, you can add a pinch of sea salt or pink sea salt to water. You can also spruce up regular water by adding a couple of slices of lemon and some fresh sprigs of mint. Make detox water at home and carry it with you.

Chapter Eight: Benefits and Drawbacks of Fasting

We have so far learned about what fasting is and how to do it in the right manner. In this chapter, let us look at the various benefits and the drawbacks of fasting.

Benefits of Fasting

There are different benefits that fasting offers. You might be wondering why you need to opt for fasting when several other diets are available. Well, the answer is quite simple, fasting is not only good for your health, but it also helps you lead a healthier life. Here are the reasons why fasting is considered to be better than other diets.

Weight Loss

Intermittent fasting oscillates between periods of eating and fasting, so your overall calorie consumption will decrease. It not only helps to restrict your calorie intake, but it also helps to maintain your weight loss. It also prevents mindless eating. When you skip a few meals, your body shifts into survival mode wherein it starts to make use of the fat that's present in your body instead of glucose to provide energy. Glucose is your primary source of energy, and when the intake of glucose reduces, your body will reach into its fat stores to supply energy. On intermittent fasting, you won't be providing your body with a constant supply of glucose, and because of this, it starts to burn fats. Also, most of the fat that is used is from the abdominal region. If you want to shed all those extra pounds piling up near your abdomen, then this is the best diet for you.

Sleep

Lack of sleep is one of the leading causes of obesity. When your body doesn't get sufficient rest, its fat burning mechanism tends to suffer. Intermittent fasting helps to regulate your sleep cycle. A good sleep cycle has several physiological benefits. It helps to elevate your overall mood and will make you feel energetic as well.

Resistance to Illnesses

Intermittent fasting assists in the growth and regeneration of cells. Did you know that your body has an internal mechanism that helps to repair damaged cells? Well, intermittent fasting helps to kickstart this process. It enhances the overall functioning of all the cells in the body, thereby improving your body's natural defense mechanism by increasing its resistance to diseases and illnesses.

A Healthy Heart

Intermittent fasting leads to weight loss, and weight loss helps to improve the cardiovascular health of your body. The buildup of plaque in your blood vessels is known as atherosclerosis. Atherosclerosis is the primary cause of several cardiovascular disorders. The thin lining of the blood vessels is known as endothelium, and a simple dysfunction of this lining causes atherosclerosis. When this lining is healthy, it prevents the deposit of plaque.

Obesity is a major problem that plagues humanity, and it is also the leading cause of the buildup of plaque in blood vessels. Stress, as well as inflammation, cause the same problem. Intermittent fasting helps to tackle the buildup of plaque and helps to fight obesity, so you can improve the health of your heart if you follow any of the protocols of fasting.

A Healthy Gut

There are millions of microorganisms present in your digestive system. No, these microorganisms aren't harmful to you. These microorganisms help to improve the overall functioning of your digestive system. They are known as the microbiome. Intermittent fasting helps to improve the health of the microbiome, and in turn, it assists to improve the health of your gut. When your gut functions optimally, it leads to better absorption of food as well. A stomach that functions well is critical to the health of a person.

Tackles Diabetes

Diabetes is a serious condition on its own; however, it is also an indication of the increase in the risk factors of several cardiovascular diseases like heart attacks or even strokes. When the level of glucose increases significantly in the bloodstream, and insulin doesn't process it, it causes diabetes. When your body becomes resistant to insulin, then it becomes quite difficult to handle glucose in the blood. Intermittent fasting helps to reduce sensitivity towards insulin, so if your body can tackle these two conditions, then you can manage diabetes successfully.

Reduces Inflammation

Whenever there is any problem in your body, the natural reaction towards the problem is inflammation. Well, it doesn't mean that all forms of inflammation are good. Inflammation can cause several health disorders like atherosclerosis, arthritis, and other neurodegenerative diseases as well. Any inflammation of this nature is known as chronic inflammation. Chronic inflammation is a painful condition, and it can restrain your body's movements as well. If you want to keep inflammation in check, then you should follow one of the intermittent fasting protocols. Inflammation causes severe pain and discomfort. If you can manage the underlying condition of inflammation, then you can successfully tackle other problems that it creates.

Promotes Cell Repair

When you fast, the cells in your body start the process of waste expulsion. Waste removal implies the breaking down of all the cells and proteins that are dysfunctional. This is known as autophagy. Autophagy also protects against several degenerative diseases like Alzheimer's and cancer.

You don't like to accumulate garbage in your house, do you? Similarly, your body shouldn't have to accumulate toxins in it either. Intermittent fasting helps to rectify this condition rather easily by kickstarting the process of cellular repair through autophagy.

Drawbacks of Fasting

Fasting is certainly not a new technique, and it has been around for a while now. It is usually used for religious and spiritual reasons, but it is steadily gaining popularity as a means of weight loss. Fasting can be a juice-only fast or even a dry fast. Fasting occasionally certainly has plenty of benefits to offer as mentioned in the previous section, but if you don't do it properly, it can be bad for your health.

Fasting can have negative effects in the short as well as

long run and can have detrimental effects on some people, including all those who want to lose weight. Ultimately, the idea of fasting, and the decision to fast, depends on the individual who wants to take up fasting. In this section, you will learn about certain drawbacks of fasting so that you can make an informed decision before you decide to start fasting.

Weight Management

According to the registered dieticians at the Mayo Clinic, it is suggested that at times fasting can be quite detrimental for weight management. After a period of fasting, it is believed that the craving for starchy and sugary foods increases and if one gives into these urges then it will certainly increase their calorie intake. Carbs are the go-to energy source for the body to provide energy.

Extreme hunger also encourages you to eat more starchy foods than usual. Ultimately, if you do succumb to this, then it will reverse the effects of fasting altogether and make the diet redundant.

If you want to manage your weight, then you need to be careful about not only what you eat, but how much you eat. Fasting is as much about the individual who is fasting as the foods that one eats.

Short-Term Side Effects

According to the reports given by the American Cancer Society, it is believed that fasting has several short-term side effects like headaches, dizziness, lightheadedness, tiredness, disruption in normal heart rhythms and even low blood pressure. All these side effects are due to the change in your diet and your body's shift to fasting.

When you eat constantly, you supply your body with a constant source of energy through glucose, but if you stop eating for short durations, then your body needs to make do with burning its internal reserves of fats to provide energy. This shift in the primary fuel for your body takes some time to get used to, and in the meanwhile, one might experience certain side effects.

People who are fasting might experience flare-ups of certain conditions like gallstones or gout. It can also impair your body's ability to absorb certain medications, and it can also alter the way your body reacts to medicines.

Therefore, I recommend that you always consult a doctor before you decide to start a new diet. There are some side effects, but with a little care and caution, you can avoid them. You will learn more about healthy ways to fast in the coming section.

Long-Term Side Effects

Fasting seems to have a detrimental impact on health in the long run as well. It can harm the immune system, and it can also have a negative effect on several organs of your body like the liver and kidneys. Fasting can also interfere with some bodily functions.

Abstaining from eating can be quite dangerous to those who are malnourished or are suffering from any preexisting health conditions. It is even possible that your body starts cannibalizing itself to provide energy if it starts to run out of stores of energy.

Dangers of Dry Fasting

While there are different methods of fasting, one method of fasting that's considered to be dangerous is dry fasting.

As I mentioned in the previous chapters about dry fasting, you will need to avoid eating and drinking anything while following this fasting protocol.

Dry fasting can lead to becoming dehydrated quite quickly, so you need to be careful. Reports from the American Cancer Society suggest that the impact of dry fasting varies from one individual to another. Different factors like heat, exertion and any compromise in health can make dry fasting quite dangerous.

People Who Should Not Fast

Well, those were the side effects of fasting, but you can quickly fix all those side effects, so no need to worry. Here is a list of people who should not attempt fasting.

Pregnant Or Nursing Women
The effect of fasting on an unborn fetus hasn't been documented and, given the importance of fetal growth, isn't recommended.

It is believed that when a woman fasts while nursing, the milk produced isn't as nutritious as it is supposed to be. There might be no difference in the amount of milk produced; however, the nutrient content in it is lessened, so current medical advice is to avoid fasting.

People With Medical Conditions
If you have any health issues related to your liver or kidney, you should not fast. If you suffer from bouts of weakness, are malnourished, anemic, frail, or exhausted, then in these cases, you should not even attempt fasting. Consult a doctor before fasting if you happen to have any medical condition.

If you are dependent on any medication, have a weak immune system, high blood pressure, or weak circulation, please consult your doctor. You can fast with a lot of conditions; however, some conditions preclude individuals from fasting.

If a person is on any medication, then the requirements of nutrition will vary. Therefore, I suggest that you must consult your physician before attempting any diet.

Eating Disorders

If you have any eating disorders such as anorexia or bulimia, you must abstain from fasting. Fasting will worsen these conditions.

After a Surgery

If you have undergone any major surgery recently, or are recovering from any major illness, then in such a case you definitely should not fast. Fasting before major surgery is forbidden too.

Afraid of Fasting

If you have a fear of fasting, then it is advisable that you don't fast. Fear doesn't put you in the right frame of mind for fasting. This can, in turn, make the experience unpleasant or even harrowing.

Fear is a strong emotion, and it can alter the physiological makeup of an individual. Therefore, it is better if you have an open mindset towards fasting. If you don't, then you'd better not try it.

Fasting Safely

Before you think about fasting, you need to know your

limits. Fasting isn't something that you just jump headfirst into without any preparation or research. Your experience, health condition, daily nutrition and the relationship you have with food need to be evaluated before you decide to start fasting.

Experience and Duration

If you are not experienced at fasting, then I recommend that you don't start with a 21-day water fast on your first attempt. You may also have found some information online that might have painted a rather rosy picture about all the benefits that you can reap by going on an extreme diet like a dry fast.

A juice cleanse is a partial fast, and it gives your body some time to get used to the idea of fasting, so I recommend that you start with a simple form of fasting before you opt for a stringent one. Also, ensure that you are aware of all the possible side effects of a fast before you start one. Start with an easy form of intermittent fasting and make your way up to an alternate day fasting plan.

One of the reasons why you must ease into fasting is to understand the way in which your body responds to fasting. If you know what you can expect, then you are in a better position to deal with issues when they come up. Being prepared for expected challenges makes it easier to fast.

Health

Forget about the saying "feed a cold, starve a fever." You need to focus on your general health and not just your immediate weight loss goals before you start fasting. If you are fasting as a means to detox your body from a junk food binge, then come up with an alternative or healthy diet plan before fasting.

You must remember that your overall health is more important than anything else that might come your way. If you are on the list of people I mentioned above, then refrain from fasting at all costs. If you don't pay attention to your health, it will land you in a lot of trouble, so please consult your doctor before you start fasting, or making any changes to your diet.

Nutrition and Hydration

Are you wondering what nutrition I am talking about while fasting? You need to understand that your body has a natural inbuilt reserve of certain key nutrients like fat-soluble vitamins that help with regular functioning of the cells when you aren't eating.

You need to ensure that your body has plenty of water-soluble mineral and vitamins while fasting. This means that you need to ensure that your body has sufficient electrolytes within it to function normally. If your body starts running out of these important electrolytes, it will lead to dehydration and will have a negative effect on your body's metabolism.

An essential form of nourishment that your body needs is water. It is not only necessary for transporting nutrients in the body, but it is also important for water removal and the regulation of your body temperature. Water provides a medium within which all other metabolic processes take place, so you need to ensure that your body is thoroughly hydrated at all times.

A lot of fasters tend to experience dehydration because their bodies aren't getting the usual volume of food and it means that they will need to make up for this deficit. The best way to do this and eliminate any of the negative effects of dehydration is to keep your body thoroughly hydrated.

Relationship with Food

All those who are experiencing any eating disorders or have suffered from any in the past need to avoid fasting until they have overcome those issues. It might seem quite appealing to fast, but it can lead to a relapse of any unhealthy condition.

If you have any history of food abuse or you use food to cope with emotional stress or trauma, then the first thing that you must do is work on developing a healthy relationship with food before you think about fasting. If you don't, then it will only lead to additional stress that is rather unnecessary.

You will learn more about the different tips that you can follow while you are fasting in the coming chapters. Each person has a different response to intermittent fasting. You will never be able to gauge how your body will react to fasting by comparing yourself to people around you.

You will need to see how your body reacts and make any changes required. What might work for one person might not work for you and that's perfectly all right. Everyone is different, so the best thing that you can do is to listen to your body. Your body knows what it wants, so learn to listen to it. Also, while you are fasting, you need to take it easy on your exercise regime for a couple of days. Give your body and yourself some time to get used to your new diet.

Chapter Nine:

Common Mistakes to Avoid

Some people tend to run into difficulty with the protocols of intermittent fasting because they adopt the wrong approach dieting. In this section, you will learn about common intermittent fasting mistakes that people make and how you can avoid them.

An Excuse to Eat Junk Food

It is quite unfortunate that people seem to think of intermittent fasting as a wonder pill that will magically solve all their health troubles. Yes, intermittent fasting is quite an effective tool that will help improve your health and help you reach your weight loss goals; however, if you decide to binge on sugar and processed foods, then this diet will not do you any good.

When you decide to follow the protocols of intermittent fasting, you need to nourish your body with whole foods. When your body is in a fasted state, then it starts to break down fats and damaged cells to provide energy. This process helps clean and heal the body. It also means that your body will be quite sensitive to all that you eat. It means that it is good if you eat food that's rich in nutrients and not indulge in any junk food cravings.

If you don't nourish your body with the nutrients it needs, then you will feel hungry - all the time! If you want to keep hunger pangs at bay, then you need to eat healthy and wholesome meals when you break your fast.

an maintain your blood sugar levels throughout the y having high-quality carbohydrates like vegetables uits along with a lot of protein and naturally fatty food. It will also help in making your body optimize its ability to burn all the stored fat. Instead of having a meal that's full of carbs, make sure you are getting all the nutrients you need and not just the calories.

Restricting Calorie Intake

The main reason why people struggle with intermittent fasting is that they try to restrict their calorie consumption when they break their fast. Read the signals your body gives you and eat until you feel full. Your body is an efficient machine, and it knows what it needs.

You need to learn to listen to your body if you want it to function properly. You needn't restrict your calorie intake. Ensure that you fill yourself up with foods that are rich in fats and fiber. If you don't consume sufficient calories, you run the risk of starvation.

Training Harder and Eating Less

If you have never tried a diet before and don't exercise regularly, then don't try to do everything at once when you start with intermittent fasting. You should never bite off more than you can chew, pun intended! You need to ease yourself, and your body, into fasting and you need to train gradually.

Don't train your body too hard and eat less. When you do this, you can cause severe damage to your health. Your body needs a little physical stress to function well, and that's why you need to exercise; however, too much exercise will unnecessarily strain your muscles and damage your health.

Obsessing Over Timings

One primary benefit of intermittent fasting is that it will help you understand your body. When you fast, you will notice a difference between real hunger and hunger caused due to stress, boredom or other factors. You need to eat when you are hungry. Don't obsess too much over the timings.

It is okay to break your fast a couple of hours early if you feel like you need to eat. Learn to listen to your body; it does know what it needs. If you cannot fast for 16 hours and had to break your fast after 12 hours, it is okay to break your fast; however, don't make it a habit of slacking off.

Not Drinking Sufficient Water

A common mistake that a lot of rookies make is that they don't drink sufficient water. Your body needs plenty of water. Water not only helps to keep hunger at bay, but it also helps the body remove toxins from within. You need to drink at least 8 (eight ounces) glasses of water daily.

Follow the tips given in this chapter to avoid common intermittent fasting mistakes and improve your chance of success.

Not Keeping yourself Busy

What will happen if someone lets you in on a secret? You will probably want to share it with others you know! Likewise, what do you think happens when you keep telling yourself to not think about eating food? You will probably want to eat everything that you set your eyes on. The more you think about food, the hungrier you will feel. Do your best to keep yourself busy.

If you are just getting started with fasting, then it is a good idea to ensure that you don't stay idle while fasting. If you keep yourself busy, you will not have any time to spare thinking about food.

Also, plan your schedule according to your fasting plan. If you avoid being around food, you will reduce the chances of being tempted to break your fast. Also, try to avoid being those who are eating. So, if you are at work while fasting, then ensure that you steer clear of the break room!

Abusing Stimulants

A lot of people who are fasting tend to have a cup of coffee instead of breakfast. It is a good idea to have about one or two cups of coffee in the morning to curb hunger and to keep hunger pangs at bay. A few cups of coffee are perfectly alright but drinking too much of coffee is a bad idea. It is diuretic in nature, and if you don't replenish the water that your body expels, then you will be severely dehydrated. It is okay to use coffee as a stimulant, but you must not abuse it.

Mindful Eating

Whenever you are breaking your fast, don't start gorging on food immediately. You shouldn't try stuffing yourself with as much food as you possibly can and instead, take a couple of minutes and let the intense hunger pass before you start eating. There is no rush, so eat slowly and avoid all sorts of distractions.

So, turn the TV off while eating and keep your phone away. Don't indulge in mindless eating and practice mindful eating. Enjoy what you are eating and indulge your senses. Don't try to compensate for the fasting period by stuffing yourself with food; you aren't doing yourself any good whatsoever.

Ease into Exercising

Your body will take about a week or so to get used to any of the intermittent fasting protocols. Once your body is used to it, you can incorporate high-intensity workouts into your exercise schedule. Working out while you are fasting will help in improving the process of weight loss by speeding up the process of burning fats for fuel generation.

However, observe caution while doing so. If you feel tired or even fatigued, you should immediately stop what you are doing. Make sure that you keep your body hydrated at all times.

Being too Ambitious

You must always start slowly. Remember that neither your body nor your mind is used to not eating for prolonged periods. It will take some time to condition yourself. You will be setting yourself up for failure if you think that you can immediately start fasting for 24 hours at a stretch. Instead, work on gradually increasing the gap between two meals. You can also begin by skipping one meal at a time.

Lack of Sufficient Sleep

Lack of sleep happens to be one of the significant obstructions to losing weight. So, make sure that you get good quality sleep at night. For optimal functioning of your body and brain, you need about 7 hours of undisturbed sleep daily.

Chapter Ten:
Don't Believe these IF Myths

Myth #1: You gain weight if you skip breakfast

By now you probably realize that breakfast isn't as important as people seem to think. It is a myth that breakfast is the most important meal of the day. It is a misconception that you will experience excessive hunger if you skip breakfast and that it leads to weight gain.

You will not put on any weight if you skip breakfast. You can fast for 24 hours and not gain any weight. Your body is designed to survive prolonged fasts, and it will not do you any harm if you skip breakfast.

Myth #2: Frequent meals improve your metabolism

Again, it is a myth that you need to eat frequently to improve your metabolism. It is not true that you can improve your body's metabolism to burn calories if you consume small and frequent meals. Your body requires little energy to digest and assimilate the food that you consume. It is known as the thermic effect, and it accounts for about 20-30% of the total calories you consume. On average, only about 10% of the total calories you consume goes towards the thermic effect of food.

You need to consider your total caloric intake and not the frequency of your meals. You don't have to eat constantly. For instance, you can have three meals worth 1000 calories each or six meals of 500 calories each, but the thermic effect accounts for about 300 calories in either of these cases, so you can fast for a prolonged period and not worry about any effect on your body's metabolism.

You need to make sure that the meals you consume are rich in dietary fats and fiber. If the meals you consume are full of carbs, not only will you feel hungry quicker, but it will also leads to weight gain. If you want to reduce your hunger, then you need a well-balanced diet. You don't have to worry about hunger pangs if you follow the protocols of fasting.

Myth #3: Small meals lead to weight loss

Small and frequent meals don't give your metabolism a boost. Small meals will not do you any good, and they will not help in weight loss. Eating frequently has the opposite of the effect you desire. You can fast for an entire day, and you don't have to worry about your metabolism.

Frequent snacking will not change your energy levels. If you worry that fasting leads to weight gain, then you can lay all those fears to rest. Your body will not burn fats to use as energy if you provide it with a constant supply of glucose.

Myth #4: The brain needs glucose, all the time

The brain needs some glucose to function; however, this doesn't mean that you need to constantly eat carbs to enable your brain to function. The brain certainly will not stop functioning if you don't eat anything for a while or if you fast for extended periods.

It is a misconception that the brain needs a lot of glucose to function. Even if you restrict your consumption of carbs, your body will burn fats to keep going. Your body starts to produce glucose through the process of gluconeogenesis. There is a reserve of glucose within the body, and the liver starts to reach into this reserve to supply glucose to your brain.

Even if you don't eat anything for 24 hours, your brain will continue to function - you don't have anything to worry about. The dietary fats present in food are broken down into ketones to provide any necessary energy. Ketones help the brain function too.

Think about all of this from an evolutionary perspective. The human race would be extinct by now if carbs were the key for survival; however, if you suffer from hypoglycemia, then you do need to snack every couple of hours to keep your blood sugar levels stable.

Myth #5: Eat often for good health

A constantly fed state is not natural for the human body. During the process of evolution, humans went through periods of starvation. If it was necessary to eat constantly to survive, we might not be alive today. Fasting induces the process of cellular repair or autophagy. Frequent snacking leads to the build-up of fats in the cells and does more harm than good.

Any belief that intermittent fasting is bad for your health is nothing more than a misconception. All the benefits that intermittent fasting provide are backed by science.

Myth #6: Your body shifts to starvation mode

Another popular misconception is that intermittent fasting switches on the starvation mode in your body. Starvation mode is when your body shuts down its metabolism to preserve calories and energy to function. It doesn't happen when you fast for short periods like you will during intermittent fasting.

When you follow the protocols of intermittent fasting, your body will produce noradrenaline, and it enables your body to burn fats and gives your metabolism a boost as well. Fasting for up to 48-hours gives your metabolism a nice boost. If you fast for longer than 48 hours in a stretch, then your body will shift into starvation mode.

Myth #7: Fasting leads to muscle loss

Intermittent fasting does not lead to muscle loss. Fasting leads to fat loss, and that's about it. Intermittent fasting allows you to develop lean muscle. When you combine this dieting protocol with the right form of exercise, then you can build muscle. Continuous restriction of calories for consecutive days together leads to muscle loss; however, you don't have to worry about all of this if you follow the protocols of intermittent fasting properly.

Myth #8: It leads to overeating

Whenever you break your fast, you might feel the urge to overeat; however, this urge passes, and you will only experience it initially until your body gets used to its new diet. Once your body is accustomed to the protocols of intermittent fasting, the urge to overeat doesn't last. Regardless of how hungry you feel, your calorie intake on intermittent fasting will be less than it usually is.

Chapter Eleven:

Frequently Asked Questions

In this section, you will find answers to all common FAQs about intermittent fasting.

How much time does your body need to get used to fasting?

It will take your body a week or two to get used to intermittent fasting. Once your body gets used to this method of dieting, you can resume your exercising schedule. Make sure that your exercising schedule isn't too stressful during the first two weeks.

What are the benefits of this diet?

Fasting has many benefits to offer that go well beyond weight loss. Fasting can help in improving your overall health and enhance the longevity of your life as well. In a recent study that was conducted to study the link between cell metabolism and fasting, it was found that fasting periodically can help in decreasing the risk of heart diseases, diabetes, aging, and so on.

Fasting is useful because, during this period, a lot of cells that are present in the body die and the stem cells start working. It starts the regeneration process and produces new cells. Other studies also show that it helps in reducing the amount of harmful cholesterol or LDL present in the blood.

Is it okay to consume certain beverages while fasting?

Yes, you can have specific beverages while fasting; however, make sure that there aren't any added calories in these drinks, so that means you will have to stay away from sodas and all sugary drinks. You can have calorie-free beverages like green tea, herbal teas, black coffee, or pretty much anything that doesn't have any calories in it.

Make sure that you drink a lot of water and that your body is thoroughly hydrated. Watch out for the extra calories in milk and sugar. It might seem like a tough call to drink your morning coffee black, but you will get used to it, especially when you start to see the benefits of your intermittent fasting regime kicking in.

Adding a bit of cream here, a spot of sugar there or even a bit of honey can have the effect of breaking the fast and sending your insulin levels back up. That means your body is not getting the full benefit of the fast.

If you are doing a 24 hour fast, keep in mind that this is only for one to two days of the week so be firm about it and push on. If you are keen on losing weight, then you must stay away from alcohol. Alcohol is rich in calories, and it leads to unnecessary calorie consumption.

If you feel like drinking, then stick to clear spirits or a glass of dry red or white wines, but that's about it. Don't overindulge on alcohol because this prevents the process of weight loss.

Can intermittent fasting be combined with any other diet?

Intermittent fasting is one of the most versatile dieting protocols ever, and it can be easily combined with other diets like the ketogenic diet and the Paleo diet.

A ketogenic diet is a low-carb and a high-fat diet in which the body produces ketones for providing energy and hence its name. The body produces ketones when there is a reduction in the consumption of carbs. When the carb consumption reduces, the body reaches into its reserves of fat for producing energy.

Intermittent fasting protocols can be easily combined with the ketogenic diet. You need to make sure that during the eating window, the food that you are consuming has a high-fat content and low or no carbs in it.

By combining intermittent fasting with any other dieting protocol, you can speed up the process of weight loss. Another diet that intermittent fasting can be efficiently combined with is the Paleo diet. The Paleo diet is a low-carb and a high-fat diet like the ketogenic diet; however, while following the Paleo diet, you will be allowed to eat only foods that our Paleolithic ancestors consumed. This diet prohibits the consumption of all grains, processed foods, sugar, and anything that human beings produce by making use of machines. By being mindful of the food that you are consuming, you can make your weight-loss more effective.

Who should not fast?

Certain people are expressly forbidden from following intermittent fasting. Pregnant women and those who are breastfeeding should not follow these dieting protocols. If you suffer from bouts of weakness, are malnourished, anemic, frail, or exhausted, then you should not fast.

Consult a doctor before fasting if you happen to have any medical condition. If you are dependent on any medication, have a weak immune system, high blood pressure, or weak circulation, please consult your doctor. If you have any eating disorders like anorexia or bulimia, you should not fast. Fasting will worsen these conditions.

Chapter Twelve: Tips and Tricks

You have been given tons of information on intermittent fasting, and your mind is probably running on overdrive! You may be worried about how you will be able to cope with the diet you are about to start. Well, stop worrying! In this chapter, you will learn about a couple of tricks that you can use while you follow intermittent fasting.

Skip Breakfast

For best results, while you follow intermittent fasting, you should fast for 14 to 16 hours daily. This means that your eating window lasts for eight to ten hours daily. You cannot achieve this unless you skip a meal daily.

Given that an average person works from 9 to 5 daily, the best meal to skip is breakfast, so your first meal will be lunch and then dinner at night.

It also means that you don't give to skip your social life because of the diet. You can plan your remaining meals according to your lifestyle. This diet offers you the necessary flexibility to do this.

No Snacks After Dinner

The purpose of a restricted eating window is to cut down on your calorie intake. Calorie deficit is the main reason for weight loss, so if you munch on additional snacks after dinner, you hinder the process of weight loss. If you eat after dinner, you will have to postpone your lunch to stick to your diet. The later you eat at night, the later you should break your fast the next day, so no more late night snacks.

Your body needs sufficient time to digest what you eat. If you eat dinner at 8 pm, your body will have adequate time to digest your food before you go to bed. If you have two tasty meals daily, you will not feel the urge to eat anything else after that.

Black Coffee Helps

Some people tend to feel hungry in the morning. Well, that's just how they are. It can be slightly tricky to overcome hunger pangs in the morning. Coffee helps to repress hunger, and you can have a cup of coffee in the morning to ease things while you fast.

Since you cannot have any calories while you fast, don't add any cream or sugar to your coffee. Start your day with a cup of black coffee. Not only does it help to make you feel fresh and energetic, it effectively suppresses your hunger as well.

Drink Lots of Water

It is good to keep your body adequately hydrated. Water also helps to cope with hunger. You should try to drink two to three liters of water while you fast. If you want, you can add lemon wedges, and some mint leaves to spruce up regular water.

Adherence

Adherence is probably the most critical tip when you follow a diet. The best diet is the one that you can follow in the long run and not just for the time being. Long-term means forever. Your diet must become a part of your lifestyle, and it must not be a temporary fad. You can probably follow a diet for a couple of months and shed 20 pounds; however, what happens when you go back to your old ways?

So, it is a good idea to follow your diet for as long as you can to maintain your weight loss and overall health. Adjust your fasting and eating windows so that it doesn't clash with your lifestyle. Also, make use of the simple recipes provided in this book to follow your diet. Make sure that there is plenty of variety to choose from, if not you will get bored of the diet.

Fast While You Work

It is easier to follow a diet when you are engaged in other activities. If you are busy with work, you won't have any time to think about your hunger. During your fasting window, keep yourself busy. Plan your fast in such a way that you will not be idle while you fast.

A portion of your fast can overlap with your work schedule, and another part can overlap with your sleep cycle. Right before the first few hours of your fast, you should consume one huge meal! Let us call this huge meal a monster meal. You will then stop worrying about when you are going to eat next! You can try sleeping a decent amount of time since you cannot worry about hunger when you are dreaming!

You need to try and keep yourself as busy as you possibly can so that you don't have time to think about what or when your next meal will be. Also, there is one other thing that you need to do. You need to keep telling yourself that you are a strong person and that you can follow this diet without giving in to any temptations.

Calories

Losing weight ultimately boils down to a calorie deficit. You need to eat fewer calories than your body burns. If you do this, you create a negative calorie balance. This basic rule applies to all forms of diets, and intermittent fasting isn't an exception. If you want, you can check your calories with any of the calorie counting apps available.

You don't have to obsess over the calories you consume. Instead, make sure that you eat sensibly and make healthy food choices. If you feel that you aren't losing any weight, then try to cut down on the calories you consume. Pay attention to whether or not the fast seems to work for you. When you consume fewer calories, that's when your body starts to burn fat.

Train Fasted

It is a good idea to train while you fast; however, it depends on the kind of exercise you perform and the duration of the exercise. Insulin levels reduce when you fast, and your body uses fat to produce energy.

Patience

Don't expect to see any miracles overnight. Intermittent fasting takes a while to work, and you cannot merely shed all those extra pounds within a day or two. It is essential that you follow the diet and don't give up on it.

Follow the IF plan for at least three weeks before you decide whether it works for you or not. If you follow it consistently, you will see positive results within the first two weeks. You also need to understand that there are many factors that will affect the way you lose weight and the amount of weight you will lose.

You have to use intermittent fasting along with other healthy habits, like exercise and sleep, to ensure that you lose weight consistently.

Have Plenty of Protein

Always make sure that you have your proteins and complex carbs before anything else. You might have something sweet or oily on your eating list; however, eating those before anything else can prove to be quite problematic. If you consume these items first, you will end up overeating. Not only are these food items rich in calories, but the amount of nutrients is minimal. All that you will end up with is a tummy ache.

It will be helpful if you plan your meals and make sure that they have got sufficient protein and complex carbohydrates them. It is likely that you will start craving for these things by the time your feeding window approaches.

Make sure that you fill yourself up with grilled chicken, lentils, or any other form of proteins, and some healthy vegetables. You can include a few carbs in the form of sweet potatoes, potatoes, a serving of rice, or something starchy. After you have had all this, there will be little or no space left for any form of junk food. Your hunger will force you to fill yourself up with the good stuff, and you won't binge on unhealthy junk.

Don't Be Too Hard on Yourself

Once in a while, you might skip a fast day or end up with a cheat meal when you break your fast. Well, you are only human and its bound to happen; however, don't be too hard on yourself and don't think of it as a failure. It is a minor hurdle, and you can overcome it. Treat it as an isolated incident. You can follow your diet for the next day. Don't worry; slip-ups are bound to happen.

There will be days when you cannot stick to your fast period and might want to break your fast sooner than usual. Doing so is okay. Also, don't feel guilty when you do this. Guilt is a stressor, and it will undo your progress. Keep an open mind towards fasting and don't be too hard on yourself. You need to get rid of thoughts about the number of hours you should fast for today.

Stop asking yourself if you should only fast for nine hours instead of ten hours! Stop worrying about how eating a single French fry during your fasting period is going to affect it. Please relax! You have a brilliant body that will adapt itself to any changes you may make to your lifestyle.

Delayed Gratification

While you fast, you might think about different foods that you will want to gorge on. When you cannot eat, that's when you start to think about different foods, so the next time you mentally salivate over certain foods, make a list. Write down all the foods that you want to eat. If you do this, you will stop thinking about the food and can instead concentrate on something else.

Don't Ignore Your Body

Each person has a different response to intermittent fasting. You will never be able to gauge how your body will react to fasting by comparing yourself to the people around you. You will need to see how your body responds and make the changes required.

Are you concerned about having lost too much muscle mass? For this, you will need to start keeping track of your strength by undertaking strength training routines to assess the intensity of your strength.

If something seems to work, stick to it. Don't ignore the signs of stress. If you feel unreasonably hungry and none of the tips help to distract you, maybe you should break your fast.

Chapter Thirteen:

5:2 Diet Meal Plan

This sample meal plan will give you a tasty and nutritious daily menu for the five non-fasting and two days of fasting. It will help you get a good idea of all that you can eat without compromising on your diet or your weight loss.

While you are following the protocols of this diet, you will be eating normally for five days of the week and then fasting for two days. On normal meal days, you should try to limit yourself to the number of calories that you need to consume to maintain your weight loss.

On the two days that you fast, you need to consume only about a quarter of the calories that you usually consume. Usually, people tend to consume anywhere between 500 to 800 calories on fasting days (women need less calories than men). You can choose any of the days that you want to fast on, but ideally, it makes sense to make sure that you aren't fasting on two consecutive days.

The 7-day meal plan for the 5:2 diet is created in such a manner that it allows you to have sufficient calories to include a couple of snacks, drinks and even treats (only on non-fasting days). The number of calories that you can eat will essentially depend on the total number of calories that you need to maintain your weight (your weight at present).

The sample plan given in this section allocates 1600 calories for all the non-fasting days. If you feel that you need more calories to maintain your weight, then you can add more snacks, drinks or even increase the portions of your meals. The calorie limit for fasting days is set at 500 calories.

If you are looking for a quick way to lose weight, then this diet is the best option for you. The 5:2 diet helps create a weekly calorie deficit of at least 3000 calories, so you will be able to lose at least one pound per week, provided that you don't go overboard on regular days.

It is a good idea to maintain a food diary to monitor the calories that you do consume on non-fasting days so that you don't go overboard. Try to do this during the first few weeks so that you get used to eating well-balanced and healthy meals. Now that you know how this diet works let us take a look at the sample plan.

Day One: Monday

The meal ideas for this day include about 1630 calories.

Breakfast: Toast with cream cheese and raspberries. Have two slices of whole-meal bread that's lightly toasted and topped with 30 grams of cream cheese and about 20 raspberries (or any other seasonal berries).

Lunch: Smoked salmon with avocado and egg salad.

Take 75 grams of mixed salad greens with three cherry tomatoes (cut them into halves), 1/4th of a red onion that's finely sliced, ½ of an avocado that's cubed, one hard-boiled egg and three slices of smoked salmon. For dressing, you can add a teaspoon of any creamy dressing like a dill dressing and sprinkle some chopped almonds on it. If you don't want to add almonds to your meal, then you can have them as a snack later on.

Dinner: Chicken Fajitas with potato wedges

You can opt for either sweet potato wedges or regular wedges. You also have the option of making these wedges at home, and if not, you can always use the readily available frozen wedges. Cook 120 grams of these wedges according to the instructions on the packet (only bake, do not fry). Make some chicken fajitas while cooking the wedges. You can make two servings of them so that you can enjoy one serving for dinner while the other one can have for a snack the following day.

I know that it can be quite challenging to transition into a new diet and at times life does get in the way. That's why this diet plan has been made as simple as possible. Whenever possible, try to cook two portions of a meal so that you can use the leftovers on the following day. For instance, if you cook two portions of chicken fajitas, you can use the leftovers for lunch or even a snack the following day.

Day Two: Tuesday

The total calories you will be consuming with these meals will be around 1578 calories.

Breakfast: Mushroom and tomato omelet with baked beans

Take two medium eggs, add a tablespoon of skimmed milk, with a little pepper and salt and beat it all together. Fry mushrooms for a minute and add the egg mixture to it and let it cook. As the eggs start to set, add three cherry tomatoes (halves) and then season it and pop it under the grill. You can serve it with half a can of baked beans on the side.

Lunch: Chicken fajita wraps

You can use the leftover chicken fajitas from Day One (either warm or cold). Place it all in a whole wheat or multigrain wrap with some lettuce, and you are good to go. You can have a banana for dessert or even have it for a snack.

Dinner: Penne with Bolognese and Parmesan

A quick Bolognese with lots of minced meat is not only easy to make, but it is also one of those recipes that you can cook in batches. You can use one portion of this sauce immediately and freeze the rest. Serve this hearty sauce with 75 grams of penne (dry weight) and garnish it with some shaved Parmesan.

According to your daily maintenance calories, you may have some spare calories that you can expand on other foods and drinks. For instance, if a person weighs 150 pounds and has a height of 5'3", then their daily maintenance calories will be 1830. If that's the case, then you can always make allowances for an extra cup of coffee with some unsweetened cream or such, or maybe you can include an extra snack to your daily meals.

Day Three: Wednesday

The third day will be your fasting day, and on all fasting days, your calorie intake must not go beyond 500 calories, so it is up to you if you want to have one large meal or maybe three very small and light meals. I feel that it is better to have three small meals spaced throughout the day so that you can keep hunger pangs at bay.

Breakfast: Whole-meal toast with peanut butter

Take one slice of wholemeal bread and toast it. Serve it with one tablespoon of peanut butter.

Lunch: Leftover Bolognese with chickpeas

Take a small serving of the Bolognese sauce you cooked and add cooked chickpeas to it. This meal ensures that you get the necessary proteins, fats and carbs necessary to keep your body going.

Dinner: Noodle soup

Make a light soup using chicken stock, and to this, you can add any of the nutrient-dense vegetables that you want to like broccoli, zucchini, peppers (not too many vegetables, maybe a handful) or you can add 50 grams of roast chicken to the broth. Have plenty of soup, it will leave you feeling fuller for longer, and you will not feel hungry. Don't add more than ten grams of noodles to this soup. Remember, it's supposed to be a light meal.

Day Four: Thursday

Don't fast on two consecutive days so that the fourth day will be a regular day and your calorie intake should not go above 1600 calories.

Breakfast: Grilled BLT sandwich

BLT is easy to make and quite tasty. Use two rashers of lean bacon, two lettuce leaves, one sliced tomato and two slices of wholemeal bread. You can add one teaspoon of mayo to bind the filling together.

Lunch: Greek salad

Make a simple Greek salad and don't forget to add some feta cheese while you're at it. You can have a banana with your lunch, or you can have it as a snack later on in the day.

Dinner: Sausage and mash

Serve three pork sausages with potato mash (make it with 200 grams of potatoes). Serve it with thick onion gravy and a bag of steamed vegetables. You can make more of the gravy and freeze it if you want.

You have the option of mixing up your meals so that you include more of the foods that you enjoy eating and cooking. If you enjoy your meals and don't get bored of them, following a diet becomes quite easy. For instance, if you like a specific dish for breakfast, then you can have the same one on multiple days. Remember that intermittent fasting is quite flexible and you can customize it according to your needs.

Day Five: Friday

The fifth day is not a fasting day, and your calorie intake will be around 1600 calories once again. Here are the different meal options that you can use.

Breakfast: Toasted bagel and soft cheese

You can have an entire bagel as long as it is made of wholemeal and not refined flour. Spread about thirty grams of cream cheese on it and enjoy your breakfast. You can add a granny smith apple to it to make it a complete meal. You can have the apple as a snack later on if you prefer.

Lunch: Jacket potatoes with cheese and beans

Bake a 200 grams potato with half a can of baked beans and serve it with thirty grams of grated cheese. You can serve it with a portion of salad made of eight grams of mixed salad leaves and 1/4th of a cucumber. You can opt for any light dressing like balsamic vinegar or even a mixture of lemon and olive oil.

Dinner: Chicken jalfrezi with rice and mango salsa

You can make two portions of this chicken curry and store it for later use. You can have one portion for dinner and the other one for lunch on the following day. Serve the curry and rice with two poppadums, for crunch, and raw mango salsa.

Day Six: Saturday

It is time to start fasting again, so your calorie intake should not go above 500 calories.

Breakfast: Porridge with raspberries

Make porridge with 30 grams of oats and 75 ml of skimmed milk along with 100 ml of water. Top off this porridge with 30 fresh raspberries or 50 fresh blueberries.

Lunch: Vegetable soup

300 grams of fresh soup will make for a filling lunch. Have plenty of broth in the soup and limit the portion of vegetables that you add to it.

Dinner: Baked cod with broccoli

Your dinner must consist of a 140 grams fillet of cod (without skin) and 80 grams of broccoli. Season it with your choice of spices and aromatics and bake it. Serve it hot with a couple of lemon wedges.

Day Seven: Sunday

Now that you are done with fasting for two days in the week, the final day of the seven-day meal plan is a regular day.

Breakfast: Spinach and tomato omelet

Two eggs with a handful of spinach and three halved cherry tomatoes make a good breakfast option. You can add 60 grams of spinach to this meal (cooked spinach). If you want, you can serve it with half a can of baked beans on the side to make it more filling.

Lunch: Chicken jalfrezi and rice

All you need to do is reheat the chicken jalfrezi curry you made previously and voila, your lunch is ready.

Dinner: Lemon sole with chips

Cook a sole fillet with lemon and pan fry it. Serve it along with 150 grams of potato fries and 80 grams of petit pois.

Remember that this was merely a sample menu. There will be days when you might not want to eat all the dishes included in a meal, so skip those bits. Perhaps you might want to eat more salad and not eat the banana as a snack, then please feel to do so. The one thing that you need to do is keep a food diary to track your food intake. Also, be a little prudent when you are curating your meals. It makes sense to eat healthy and well-balanced meals if you want to lose weight. If you don't do this, then all the effort that goes into fasting will do you no good.

Chapter Fourteen:

16:8 Sample Menu

While following the 16:8 protocol of intermittent fasting, you must ensure that you are fasting for 16 hours in a day with an eating window of eight hours, so during those eight hours, you must ensure you are eating sufficient food that will keep you going throughout the fasting period while ensuring that your body gets all the nutrients that it needs.

For instance, if you decide to take up this fasting protocol and your first meal is at 10 am, then your last meal must be at no later than 6 p.m. in the evening. Here is a sample menu of what a typical weekly menu will look like in this diet.

Day One: Monday

Breakfast: Fat burning coconut cookies loaded with nuts.

Add any nuts that you want, but don't eat more than a handful of nuts per day.

Lunch: Teriyaki zucchini noodles with any lean protein like chicken or fish.

Dinner: Honey and garlic shrimp.

You are free to add a small portion of salad with a light dressing if you want.

Day Two: Tuesday

Breakfast: Low-carb pancakes with a handful of berries.

Lunch: Grilled chicken with curry and cauliflower rice.

Dinner: Chicken and broccoli stir-fry.

Day Three: Wednesday

Breakfast: Turmeric milkshake with a handful of nuts.

Lunch: Cumin-spiced beef lettuce wraps.

Dinner: Miso soup with a protein of your choice.

Day Four: Thursday

Breakfast: Low-calorie eggcups with a variety of toppings like bacon, ham, vegetables and cheese.

Lunch: Triple berry spinach salad with candied pecans.

Dinner: Blackened salmon with an avocado salsa.

Day Five: Friday

Breakfast: Bacon spaghetti squash fritters.

Lunch: Crispy and flaky fish tacos with all fixings.

Dinner: Turkey meatball and kale soup.

Day Six: Saturday

Breakfast: Green smoothie made of avocados, spinach and any other greens of your choice with honey.

Lunch: Smokey green bean turkey skillet.

Dinner: Buttered cod in a skillet.

Day Seven: Sunday

Breakfast: Cinnamon rolls made of whole grain flour and natural sweetener instead of sugar.

Lunch: Carnitas burrito bowl with all fixings.

Dinner: Roasted lemon butter shrimp with asparagus on the side.

Time	Description
Midnight	Sleeping and fasting
4 a.m.	Sleeping and fasting
8 a.m.	Fasting
10 a.m.	Break the fast
12 p.m.	Lunch time
6 p.m.	Dinner and then fasting starts
Midnight	Fasting period

Chapter Fifteen:

One Meal a Day Sample Plan

In this section, you will learn about the One Meal a Day food plan. With this form of intermittent fasting, instead of having three meals in a day, you will be consuming one large meal and you will need to consume it within a one to two-hour eating window, so you will be fasting for over 20 hours in a day with this method of intermittent fasting.

If you are following this protocol and if you think that you can eat whatever you want, then you will be facing several nutrient deficiencies.

Technically, this isn't a diet and it is more of a strategy of eating. Technically, you are free to eat anything that you want on a one meal a day diet, but it is not recommended.

Take a moment to think about it, if you fast for 22 hours in a day and then binge on a pint of ice cream, it wouldn't make any sense to fast in the first place. You might be able to meet the daily caloric requirement, but your body doesn't get any of the nutrients that it needs for sustenance. If you do this, you will be doing your body more harm than good.

Since you will be eating only one meal in a day, you need to make sure that the meal counts. You must ensure that there is plenty of diversity in the food you eat and that you are consuming foods that are rich in nutrients.

Let me take you through the OMAD food pyramid so that

you have a better understanding of the foods that you should include in your daily diet. While planning for a meal, you must start with the first level and slowly make your way through the food pyramid.

Level One: High-Fiber Vegetables

This is where you will be eating a bulk of your meal. You need to focus on foods that are nutrient dense, so the vegetables that you can include in your diet are kale, spinach, Brussels sprouts, broccoli, cucumber, peppers and squash. Squash includes summer squash, zucchini, and the likes. You can include all forms of cruciferous vegetables. Squash is not only a high-fiber vegetable, but certain types of it also fall under the category of carb-based foods.

Level Two: Fats and Oils

A lot of people aren't really aware of the difference between good and bad fats or oils. People tend to use hydrogenated oils and these oils increase inflammation in the body and are unhealthy. You need to consume good quality fats and oils. Saturated fats include lard, tallow, chicken fat, duck fat, goose fat, ghee, butter, coconut oil, avocado oil, macadamia oil and olive oil. You can also include some cheese in your diet.

Apart from this, other sources of healthy fats are nuts. Macadamia nuts, pecans, almonds, walnuts, sunflower seeds, pine nuts, flaxseeds, pumpkin seeds, sesame seeds, and hemp seeds. You can also have a small quantity of Brazil nuts.

You should not overconsume nuts and seeds as they can overburden your gut. Ensure that the nuts and seeds that you consume are in raw form and aren't roasted.

Level Three: Proteins

When you are thinking about proteins, opt for organic and grass-fed meats as much as you can. Grass-fed meats include beef, duck, lamb, goat, and venison, fish caught in the wild (salmon, trout, mahi mahi and sardines), pork, poultry, eggs and offal (only if it is grass-fed).

Level Four: Carbohydrates

What is the first thing that pops into your head when you think about carbs? Is it bread, spaghetti, any other form of pasta and pizza? Well, these are carb-based foods, but let me remind you once again, you need to consume healthy foods. You must opt for nutrient-dense carbs like sweet potatoes, beans, peas, tomatoes, butternut squash and such.

Level Five: Low-Glycemic Index Foods

You need to focus on low-glycemic foods. It is the final tier of the food pyramid but is as important as all the other tiers. If you are consuming a diet that's high in sugar while on OMAD, it will give you a false sense of satiety. It might make you feel full for a while, but once your body absorbs all that sugar, you will feel hungry again. You must not eat fruits that are high in sugar on OMAD. Examples of low-glycemic foods are all types of berries like strawberries, blueberries, raspberries and blackberries, Granny Smith apples and grapefruit.

Now that you know what you can and cannot include in your diet, the next step is to plan a sample menu for yourself. What do all these different levels look like when you combine them together?

Meal One: Monday

- A bowl of chili made of mixed beans and vegetables topped with an avocado.

- Chicken fajitas with all the fixings like guacamole, sour cream, lettuce, even taco shreds and cheese.

- For dessert, you can have a chocolate coconut mousse that's topped with a handful of berries. It might sound like a big meal, but with OMAD, it needs to be a big meal.

Meal Two: Tuesday

- Vegetable minestrone soup along with a side of a summer salad with an olive oil dressing. Grain-free biscuits with grass-fed butter.

- Spaghetti squash along with meatballs and sauce.

- For dessert, you can have unsweetened whipped cream and some berries.

Meal Three: Wednesday

- Peanut butter overnight oats with a ginger and turmeric smoothie.
- A bowl of avocado salad with carrot ginger dressing.
- Mexican lentil tortilla soup.

Meal Four: Thursday

- Whole-wheat veggie taco.
- A salmon fillet with some pesto and a handful of almonds.
- For dessert, you can have a creamy peppermint shake.

Meal Five: Friday

- Asparagus soup with a Greek salad (don't forget the feta).
- BBQ pork chops along with a small portion of baked sweet potatoes or one serving of Cajun-spiced rice.
- For dessert, you can have a hazelnut and avocado pudding topped with chia seeds.

Meal Six: Saturday

- Lamb stew with tomatoes and peppers along with

a portion of a salad with mixed greens and a fatty dressing.

- For dessert, you can have nutty fudge (make sure that you add natural sweeteners and not sugar).

Meal Seven: Sunday

- Garlic roasted lamb with a zesty arugula and tomato salad (crumble any cheese of your choice as a topping).

- For dessert, have a honey and date pudding with a small serving of unsweetened whipped cream.

Here is what an ideal One Meal a Day Diet looks like during a week.

Time	Description
Midnight	Sleeping and fasting
4 am	Sleeping and fasting
8 am	Fasting
Until Noon	Fasting
4 pm	Fasting
8 pm	Feeding window
Midnight	Fasting period

Conclusion

I want to thank you again for choosing this book!

So, there you have it! All the information that you need to know about autophagy and intermittent fasting is provided in this book. Now you know for sure that not eating for prolonged periods of time will not do your body any harm.

In fact, it does your body a whole lot of good. The trick to making the most of intermittent fasting is to eat correctly! It isn't about the food you eat, but when you eat that counts; however, it doesn't mean that you can eat all sorts of junk.

Make sure that you eat healthy foods during your eating interval, and you are good to go. Have plenty of fluids during the fasting period and don't allow your body to get dehydrated.

There are various benefits that intermittent fasting offers. Not just that, there are different variations of intermittent fasting that you can try as well. If you feel that one doesn't work for you, try another method. The protocols of intermittent fasting are quite simple, and it doesn't have any complicated guidelines.

Well, the next step is to get started with this diet. The different tips mentioned in this book will help you to follow and stick to your diet.

Autophagy is a natural process, and by following any of the different methods of intermittent fasting, you can kickstart this process, so all that you need to do now is select a method of intermittent fasting and get started with it!

And lastly, if you found the book informative, I request you to recommend it to your friends and family.

Thank you and all the best!

Resources and Further Reading

https://drmindypelz.com/the-benefits-of-dry-fasting/

http://siimland.com/what-can-you-drink-while-fasting/

https://blog.bulletproof.com/autophagy-for-longevity-detoxification/

https://www.nobelprize.org/prizes/medicine/2016/press-release/

https://www.naomiwhittel.com/the-12-important-benefits-of-autophagy/

https://perfectketo.com/16-8-intermittent-fasting-ketosis/

https://healthyeating.sfgate.com/disadvantages-fasting-5546.html

https://www.globalhealingcenter.com/natural-health/how-to-fast-safely-considerations-before-fasting/

https://www.medicalnewstoday.com/articles/320125.php

https://www.healthline.com/nutrition/the-5-2-diet-guide

https://www.weightlossresources.co.uk/diet/plans/5-2-diet-7-day-meal-plan.htm